Education in America

Education in America

GEORGE CHARLES ROCHE III

The Foundation for Economic Education, Inc.
Irvington-on-Hudson, New York   •   1969

The Author and Publisher

DR. GEORGE CHARLES ROCHE III formerly taught history and philosophy at the Colorado School of Mines. He is a member of the staff and Director of Seminars at the Foundation for Economic Education. Among his writings are booklets on *American Federalism* and *Power.* Scheduled for 1969 publication by Arlington House is his history of the development of our Western heritage of freedom, modern departures from it, and prospects for a restoration.

THE FOUNDATION FOR ECONOMIC EDUCATION is an educational champion of private ownership, the free market, the profit and loss system, and limited government. It is nonprofit and nonpolitical. Sample copies of the Foundation's monthly journal, *The Freeman,* as well as a list of books and other publications, are available on request.

Published July 1969
Copyright 1969 by George Charles Roche III
Standard Book Number 910614-21-0
Printed in the United States of America

Preface

INCREASING NUMBERS of Americans express concern over the deterioration of modern society, accurately pinpointing various failings—social, political, and economic. Most of us are far better at discovering shortcomings than describing solutions. As the result, conversations on the American decline usually conclude with the following argument: Since society can be no better than the level of understanding displayed by its individual members, and since the individual's understanding is based largely upon his educational experience, we can only arrest the national decline by "more education."

I do not fault the argument as far as it goes, but the specific definition of "more education" seems open to question. Much of what passes for "education" today seems calculated to yield a product totally different from the properly educated individual. The sort of moral leadership required if our civilization is to endure must spring from vastly different premises than those which now dominate educational institutions.

This book came into existence as an attempt to examine some of the ideas which today so hamper our educational endeavors. Hopefully it also provides some definition of the proper educational values which should be substituted.

Thanks are due many people for ideas and encouragement, but are especially called for in the case of Mrs. Muriel Brown, who provided great encouragement and secretarial assistance at every stage of the research and writing, and Dr. Paul L. Poirot, for editorial assistance as these chapters were first serialized in *The Freeman*.

GCR III

Table of Contents

1. What Has Happened?

IN WHAT MUST SURELY BE his most quoted remark, the nineteenth century novelist, Thomas Peacock, commented that anyone talking about education was the bore of all bores since his subject lacked a beginning, a middle, or an end. Anyone attempting to write on the subject would seem, therefore, to undertake a difficult assignment. Yet, what other topic has had so much written about it, so little of which is read? With his usual blunt Yankee insight, Emerson summed up the current attitude on such treatises:

> It is ominous, a presumption of crime, that this word Education has so cold, so hopeless a sound. A treatise on education, a convention for education, a lecture, a system, affects us with slight paralysis and a certain yawning of the jaws.

I know what Emerson meant, yet must risk that slight paralysis and yawning of the jaws in my reader. Why? Because it seems painfully clear that our society is breaking down rather than maturing and because this trend seems likely to continue until we face and correct certain fundamental misconceptions in our educational framework.

In the last century, men of good will seemed naively confident that the mere communication of knowledge could change the world. All problems, all social difficulties, could be corrected if only ignorance could be conquered. Unfortunately, knowledge and ignorance are at best highly relative terms. The problem is further aggravated when we ask the question, "Knowledge and ignorance of what?" Sadly enough, that issue was all too seldom faced when we were constructing the philosophy and institutions of modern American education.

The Mixed Blessings of Universal Education

Following the lead of the nineteenth century, modern America and most other nations of the Western world have established universal institutionalized education. However, there are some signs that ignorance has not yet been vanquished. There also are signs that such knowledge as has been imparted has brought little progress toward "the good society." Worst of all, there are signs that teaching everyone to read may be less than an unmixed blessing:

> . . . teaching everyone to read opens minds to propaganda and indoctrination at least as much as to truths; and on political and social matters it is propaganda and indoctrination rather than truth that universal education has most conspicuously nurtured.[1]

Modern dictators have made very effective use of universal institutionalized education.

As universal education has failed to provide the utopia ex-

---

[1] James Burnham, *Suicide of the West,* pp. 138-139.

pected of it, the Western world in general, and the United States in particular, has begun to suspect that even our advanced, literate, "modern" civilization on which we so pride ourselves may prove to be mortal after all. We are beginning to suspect that civilizations can die as well as grow. Moreover, we are becoming restive as we see some of the signs of decay around us. We are beginning to suspect that there are other obstacles blocking our path to an ideal society, obstacles derived from the human condition, obstacles not easily overcome by merely providing larger and larger schools, more and more books, and more and more of all the other trappings of universal institutionalized education. The differences we note between an "educated man" and a "good man" should cause us to re-examine what we mean when we use the word "education."

Surely, education should be helpful rather than harmful. Surely, education should be encouraged to the utmost. At least this is the way we all talk about the subject. Do we really mean it? More important, should we really mean it? The answer to these questions depends on what sort of "education" we have in mind.

Perhaps the most "educated" people of antiquity were the Greeks, yet they destroyed themselves. The Germans have been among the most literate and most completely "educated" people of modern times, yet succumbed to the siren song of an Adolf Hitler. Despite the fact that much of what passes for "education" produces undesirable results in whole nations, despite the results it has been producing lately among many well-endowed young people within our

own society, we still find in the minds of most people that
"more education" is the answer to all problems.

An alarming percentage of our citizens, it is to be
feared, stop with the word "education" itself. It is for
them a kind of conjuror's word, which is expected to work
miracles by the very utterance. If politics becomes self-
ish and shortsighted, the cure that comes to mind is "education." If juvenile delinquency is rampant, "education"
is expected to provide the remedy. If the cultural level of
popular entertainment declines, "education" is thought of
hopefully as the means of arresting the downward trend.
People expect to be saved by a word when they cannot
even give content to the word.[2]

Shortchanging the Students

Twentieth century America is a society in which all children go to school. Yet, today our cities are populated by
children worse behaved and more socially dangerous than
the less "educated" youngsters of former times. Let me
hasten to insist that I am not against children learning to
read. In fact, one of the complaints which can be leveled
against modern education is that large numbers of high
school graduates are scarcely able to read and quite unable
to write a coherent paragraph.

It is not that our young people have been underexposed to
"education," but rather that they have been badly short-
changed in what they have received. Meanwhile, many of
our high school and college graduates who have learned to

---

[2] Richard Weaver, *Life Without Prejudice,* p. 42.

read have then been condemned to spend their time with books and lectures calculated to undercut those human values that make for the good society. The resultant generations of young people with little or no knowledge of the nature of man, and a scarcely better understanding of the economics, politics, and social concepts that have been produced by the great thinkers of the Western world, continue to pour from our "educational"system. Surely, these young people cannot be blamed for the direction of our society. Surely, a system which produces young people, some of whom cannot read, many of whom cannot think, and most of whom lack knowledge of their own heritage and the moral values which underlie it, is a system which needs serious attention. We have been pouring unlimited amounts of money into the mechanics of the education of our young. Perhaps it is time we began to devote a little thought to the subject as well.

Meanwhile, we Americans seem to have almost no idea what to do with our children. School, in many cases, seems to be a convenient place to file our young people until the draft boards or the labor unions absorb them. As parents and future employers, it appears that at least a part of our concern for more and more years of "education" is to get the youngsters off our minds. This seems to be evidenced by more preschool education, by the extension of the high school years through the thirteenth and fourteenth grades at junior colleges, by our assumption that nearly all young people should now attend at least four years of college, and more and more of these same people attend graduate school as well. In the process we have cheapened the bachelor's degree to a level inferior to what an eighth grade diploma once constituted and we have made the Ph.D. degree a mere license to teach. "What price education?"

Surely, American education suffers from an almost unbelievable amount of aimlessness and confusion. We spend more on our educational institutions than have most societies past or present. Yet, as our buildings grow larger and larger, the graduates from them seem to be less and less prepared, in either mind or character, for carrying on our civilization. It is widely assumed, and correctly so, that our prospects as a nation and as a civilization rest upon our ability to inculcate skills and civilized values in our young people. Such a task is so important that our society cannot any longer afford to let it drift as it has been drifting. As one critic has suggested, "Is it possible that 'education' is too important to be left to the educators?"

Of course, it's possible to lightly dismiss such questions. Criers of doom are always warning that the end of civilization is in sight, but the sun usually seems to rise the next morning. Isn't it true that in our developing technology and in our scientific achievements we have been advancing steadily? Isn't it true that we have more material possessions than any other civilization, past or present? Yes, but it also is true that history is filled with the records of dead and dying civilizations; civilizations which in most cases achieved the greatest bloom of prosperity and self-satisfaction at the very time when they had so lost their way, and so departed from the very values which gave them direction, that their own decline and decay had already begun, unnoticed by most people.

There are usually on the scene some people able to sense the turn of events; but Jeremiahs seldom get a good press in their own society. People don't like to be told such things. One of the warnings concerning our own failing as a civilization comes to us, however, from a man well publicized throughout the Western world. In 1923, Albert Schweitzer commented in his *Civilization and Ethics:*

> My subject is the tragedy of the Western world-view. . . .
> Our civilization is going through a severe crisis. . . . Most
> people think that the crisis is due to the war but they are
> wrong. The war, with everything connected with it, is
> only a phenomenon of the condition of uncivilization in
> which we find ourselves.

Our "uncivilization" was attributed by Schweitzer to the great gap which has opened up between our material and spiritual understanding. He sensed that modern man was becoming dependent upon larger and larger economic, social, and political aggregations of power. He warned that, in the process, the individual man was finding it increasingly difficult to identify and establish his own personality. American education serves as a prime example of modern man's emphasis upon the material rather than the spiritual, an emphasis upon larger and larger aggregations of collective authority and organization within which individual personality finds a smaller and smaller place. Let anyone who doubts this attend the massive public high school or gigantic state university campus of his choice. What we teach and how we teach it makes it harder and harder for the individual to find and defend his place in the sun.

Progress and Regress

This peculiar composite of material progress and spiritual regress leads us directly to one of the dichotomies of our age. While technicians and scientists radiate optimism in their prediction of a glorious future, most of the popular writers of our time, concerned with the human condition, view the present as an absurd joke and see the future as hopeless. All too many modern writers see the universe and human life as essentially meaningless. If anyone might doubt such a sweeping statement, let him consider the literature which our young people read today in the high schools and colleges of America. The same overwhelming impression of the meaninglessness of human life can be detected in conversation with many young people, or in even a casual perusal of the press and theater of our time.

It may be that in our pursuit of "education" we have been pursuing the wrong ideas. Our American educational system might be compared to the glorious promise of the nineteenth century frontier roads leading to the West. They offered a majestic appearance as they left the East, with planted rows of trees on either side to tempt the traveler. But, as Emerson remarked, they soon became narrower and narrower and ended in a squirrel track running up a tree. There are some signs that, for all of our grand hopes and great expenditure, our institutional educational framework may likewise be leading us up a tree.

Over 2,300 years ago, Aristotle stated the question most succinctly: "Consideration must be given to the question, what constitutes education and what is the proper way to be educated?" The answer appears to be one for which Western man is still searching. Perhaps it is time to remind ourselves of historian Herbert Butterfield's injunction:

> Amongst historians, as in other fields, the blindest of all the blind are those who are unable to examine their own pre-suppositions, and blithely imagine therefore that they do not possess any. . . . It must be emphasized that we create tragedy after tragedy for ourselves by a lazy un-examined doctrine of man which is current amongst us and which the study of history does not support.

Professor Butterfield would get little hearing for his remarks throughout much of the academic community today. Still, he may be right. We may have become so busy discussing "education" with the current clichés and shallow value judgments which we have come to accept, that we are over-looking some philosophic and institutional flaws of grave magnitude. Perhaps the time has come for a serious and sustained effort in thinking through the goals and means of American education. It is past time for all of us to become interested in the subject, especially since educators in many cases respond to criticism "by re-doubling their efforts and forgetting their aims," as Robert Hutchins has said. Surely, we can do better.

Actually, this soul searching and re-examination of American education has been under way in this country ever since World War II. Many people are deeply concerned about various practical or philosophic aspects of one level or another of American education. But no single level of education can be considered in a vacuum. The students of colleges are, after all, the graduates of American high schools. The teachers of high schools are the graduates of American colleges and universities. Not only are various levels of American education interrelated, but the practical and philosophic aspects of the problem feed back upon one another to produce a complex of relationships which deserves a careful treatment within the compass of a single study.

Aspects of the Problem

Some of the problems we will be examining in an effort to achieve an improved understanding of American higher education will include:

(1) What should we be trying to teach? What is the nature of the underlying moral framework which society must pass from one generation to another for its own self-preservation?

(2) How does education fail when it departs from such an underlying moral framework? What have been the results of such a departure in our own society?

(3) What of the problems of size and the problems of population which confront our schools with overcrowding, lowering of standards, and many related difficulties?

(4) Why is it that child-centered education, education essentially *without discipline,* is a disaster, both for the child and for the society in which he is to assume a role?

(5) What of the role played by the educationists and the largely dominant philosophy currently pursued in American education?

(6) What of the failures in higher education, stemming from institutional inertia, excessive specialization, the committee mentality, the "publish or perish" syndrome, and the other shortcomings of the college and university community?

(7) What of the college revolts of our age? Who is responsible: student, faculty, or society? More important, where do we go from here?

(8) What of the problem of public versus private financing and philosophy for all levels of American education?

This listing of vital questions concerning American education could be extended. What of the public and private roles in research and technology? What of the problem of vocational training? What involvement should private industry have in this question? What are the wellsprings of that human creativity which has allowed society to advance as far as it has and how can those sources best be safeguarded within our educational system? What of the many good jobs being done by good people on various levels of American education and how can they best be preserved in a revamped system? And finally, what sort of a philosophy of education could best provide for America the trained, disciplined, truly human, young people so desperately needed if our nation and the Western world are to survive?

An attempt to answer all of these questions is, of course, ambitious. But such a task is made far easier by all the modern critiques of education on its various levels which have been undertaken by so many highly qualified people. Even more important, the whole rationale for a proper philosophy of education derives from a large number of distinguished thinkers, past and present, who have perceived the basic truth that how a civilization deals with its young and creative minds is the final key to the future of that civilization.

With a tip of our hat toward all those better men who have gone before, let us examine some of the problems of American education.

2. Freedom, Morality, and Education

To fully appreciate the shortcomings of our present educational framework and face realistically the task of rebuilding it requires a careful and complete understanding of the concepts we value in society—a "thinking through" of our own first principles. What kind of educational goals do we really desire?

To Plato, proper education of the young consisted in helping them to form the correct mental habits for living by "the rule of right reason." But, how do we define right reason?

An important part of education centers on the attempts of society to transmit its culture to the rising generation. What are the accomplishments of past generations? What have been the goals and values by which society has lived? What guidelines should be available to the rising generation as it faces its own inevitable problems?

Still, education must be far more than the mere indoctrination of the young into the methods of the past. A hallmark of Western civilization is its educational focus upon the development of the individual's capacity to function as an individual, tempered by recognition of the common characteristics imposed upon all civilized communities by the unchanging aspects of human nature. In this sense, the proper goal of education is everywhere the same: improve the individual as an individual, stressing the peculiar and unique attributes each has to develop, but also emphasizing the development of that "higher side" shared by all men when true to their nature. This educational goal might be described as the quest for "structured freedom," freedom for the individual to choose *within* a framework of values, values universal to *all* men simply because they are human beings.

A Framework of Values

Education in this best sense requires no elaborate paraphernalia. It is characterized, not by elaborate classrooms or scientific "methods," but by an emphasis upon the continuity and changelessness of the human condition. The effort to free the creative capacities of the individual, to allow him to become truly himself, must recognize the values which past generations have found to be liberating, asking that each new generation make the most of inherited values while striving to enrich that heritage. True education is society's attempt to enunciate certain ultimate values upon which individuals, and hence society, may safely build. The behavior of children toward their parents, toward their responsibilities, and even toward the learning process itself is closely tied to such a framework of values.

✓ Thus, in the long run, the relationship we develop between teacher and pupil, the type of learning we encourage, the manner in which we organize our school systems, in short, the total meaning we give to the word "education," will finally be determined by our answers to certain key questions concerning ultimate values.

Those who built the Western world never questioned this continuity of our civilization nor attempted to pluck out the threads that run through its fabric. Ever since the Hebrews and Greeks made their great contributions to Western thought, it has been taken for granted that through the life of the mind man can transcend his physical being and reach new heights. Self-realization, discipline, loyalty, honor, and devotion are prevailing concepts in the literatures, philosophies, and moral precepts that have shaped and mirrored Western man for centuries.[1]

The necessity for such an underlying value system has been well established in the work of such eminent social critics of our age as C. S. Lewis and Richard Weaver. The case for such an underlying system must not depend upon the whims of debate with the relativistic, subjectivist spokesmen who today dominate so much of American education and thought. Those who hold that certain civilized values are worthy of transmission to the young, that some standards are acceptable and others are not, are on firm ground in their insistence that such values and standards must be the core of any meaningful educational framework.

The late C. S. Lewis, an urbane and untiring critic of the intellectual tendencies of the age, used the word *Tao* to convey the core of values and standards traditionally and

---

[1] Thomas Molnar, *The Future of Education,* p. 30.

universally accepted by men, in the Platonic, Aristotelian, Stoic, Christian, and Oriental frameworks. The *Tao* assumes a fixed standard of principle and sentiment, an objective order to the universe, a higher value than a full stomach. As such, the *Tao* presupposes standards quite incompatible with the subjective, relativist suppositions of "modern man." We are told by the relativists that the *Tao* must be set aside; the accumulated wisdom of centuries, the values of East as well as West, of Christian and non-Christian, the striving of the past to discover the higher side of man and man's conduct, must not stand in the path of "progress." Thus, the "revolt" of the "Now Generation."

Advances in technology account in part for the denial of our heritage. Since scientific and technological knowledge tends to accumulate (i.e., be subject to empirical verification as correct or incorrect, with the correct then added to the core of previously verified knowledge), many people assume that man's scientific progress means he has outgrown his past and has now become the master of his own fate. Moral questions are of a different order. Wisdom, not science or technology, points the way for progress here. For an individual to be inspired by the wisdom and moral rectitude of others, he must first make such wisdom his own. This is education in its finest sense.

To grasp the accumulated moral wisdom of the ages is to become habituated to such concerns and to their claims upon one's personal conduct. At that point, the rule of right reason, the goal which Plato set for education, becomes the guiding light of the individual.

This rule of right reason could provide the frame of reference so lacking in today's society. Many modern existentialists complain that the world is meaningless and absurd. It is not surprising that the world no longer has meaning for those who recognize none but materialistic values. The world of reason and freedom, the real world in which it matters a great deal what the individual chooses to do, is revealed only in the spiritual quality of man that so many moderns deny. It is this higher spiritual quality of the individual, evidenced in his creative capacity to choose, which alone can give meaning to life and transform the world of the individual. This is the recognition of those higher values that lead to Truth. Such an awareness on the part of the individual, such a rule of right reason, will be, in Berdyaev's words ". . . the triumph of the realm of spirit over that of Caesar. . . ." This triumph must be achieved anew by each individual as he strives for maturity . . . and his struggle for maturity constitutes the educative process.

A Higher Law

Despite our vaunted "modern breakthroughs in knowledge," it is doubtful that anyone now alive possesses more wisdom than a Plato, an Epictetus, a Paul, or an Augustine. Yet much of what passes for "education" in our time either denies this accumulation of past wisdom or belittles it in the eyes of the student. Truth, after all, is a measure of *what is,* a measure of an infinite realm within which the individual is constantly striving to improve his powers of perception. As the individual draws upon his heritage and applies self-discipline, he comes to recognize more and more of that truth and to understand it. The individual is thus able to find himself and his place in the universe, to become truly free, by recognizing a fixed truth, a definite right and wrong, not subject to change by human whim or political dictate. The individual can only be free when he serves a higher truth than political decree or unchecked appetite.

Such a definition of freedom in consonance with a higher law has its roots deep in the consciousness of civilized man.

In early Hinduism that conduct in men which can be called good consists in conformity to, or almost participation in, the *Rta*—that great ritual or pattern of nature and supernature which is revealed alike in the cosmic order, the moral virtues, and the ceremonial of the temple. Righteousness, correctness, order, the *Rta,* is constantly identified with *satya* or truth, correspondence to reality. As Plato said that the Good was "beyond existence" and Wordsworth that through virtue the stars were strong, so the Indian masters say that the gods themselves are born of the *Rta* and obey it.

The Chinese also speak of a great thing (the greatest thing) called the *Tao.* It is the reality beyond all predicates, the abyss that was before the Creator Himself. It is Nature, it is the Way, the Road. It is the Way in which the universe goes on, the Way in which things everlastingly emerge, stilly and tranquilly, into space and time. It is also the Way which every man should tread in imitation of that cosmic and super-cosmic progression, conforming all activities to that great exemplar. "In ritual," say the Analects, "it is harmony with Nature that is prized." The ancient Jews likewise praise the Law as being "true."[2]

Thus, the Christian insistence that man must order his affairs according to a higher law is far from unique. Such a view has been held in common by all civilized men. Our own early institutions of higher learning were deeply committed to the transmission of such a heritage. The nine colleges founded in America in the seventeenth and eighteenth centuries, (Harvard, Yale, Brown, Dartmouth, Columbia, Princeton, Pennsylvania, Rutgers, and William and Mary) were all of religious origin. Such was the early American view of education.

Human Freedom and the Soul of Man

There is a measure of truth in the Grand Inquisitor's assertion that many people do not wish to be free. Freedom can be painful, and someone like the Grand Inquisitor usually is at hand, quite willing to take over the chore of making decisions for others. Those civilizations which have prospered, however, have been peopled by those who appreciated the transcendent importance of their individuality and who valued the freedom necessary for its expression and fulfillment. "Education is not, as Bacon thought, a means of showing people how to get what they want; education is an exercise by means of which enough men, it is hoped, will learn to want what is worth having."[3]

---

[2] C. S. Lewis, *The Abolition of Man*, pp. 27-28.
[3] "Science and Human Freedom," *Manas*, Feb. 28, 1968, p. 7.

Education is an exercise by which men will learn to want
what is worth having. This is a recurrent idea among Western thinkers. Aristotle wrote that the proper aim of education was to make the pupil like and dislike the proper things.
Augustine defined the proper role of education as that which
accorded to every object in the universe the kind and degree of love appropriate to it. In Plato's *Republic,* the well-
educated youth is described as one . . .

> who would see most clearly whatever was amiss in ill-
> made works of man or ill-grown works of nature, and
> with a just distaste would blame and hate the ugly even
> from his earliest years and would give delighted praise
> to beauty, receiving it into his soul and being nourished
> by it, so that he becomes a man of gentle heart. All this
> before he is of an age to reason; so that when Reason at
> length comes to him, then, bred as he has been, he will
> hold out his hands in welcome and recognize her be-
> cause of the affinity he bears to her.

What is this higher side of human nature which can be
cultivated, this higher side of man which will learn to want
what is worth having? According to the standards of Western civilization, it is the human soul.

If we seek the prime root of all this, we are led to
the acknowledgment of the full philosophical reality of
that concept of the soul, so variegated in its connota-
tions, which Aristotle described as the first principle of
life in any organism and viewed as endowed with supra-
material intellect in man, and which Christianity revealed
as the dwelling place of God and as made for eternal
life. In the flesh and bones of man there exists a soul

which is a spirit and which has a greater value than the whole physical universe. Dependent though we may be upon the lightest accidents of matter, the human person exists by the virtue of the existence of his soul, which dominates time and death. It is the spirit which is the root of personality.[4]

Our Choices Affect Our Lives

Some of those who espouse the idea of freedom are quick to declaim such terms as soul, God, or Higher Law, feeling that such "mysticism" denies the individual the capacity to freely choose since it binds him to a higher Authority. This is a groundless fear. In fact, the whole idea of a higher law and a God-given capacity for individual free choice only opens the door into a world in which man is constantly remaking the world as he modifies and expands his own horizons. It is precisely the fact that the soul of the individual derives from a higher order of nature that allows man to constantly remake the world and his own life according to his own understanding and his own perception. This is the source of the self-discipline which produces honor, integrity, courage, and the other attributes of civilized man. This is the source of the framework within which all meaningful, civilized choice takes place.

Still, the existentialists may be right about one point. It is true that man finds himself encased within a body and a material existence which he did not choose. It is also true that he finds himself limited by the ideas peculiar to his

---

[4] Jacques Maritain, *Education at the Crossroads,* p. 8.

time. Even if he chooses to fight such ideas, the very nature of that choice and struggle is determined by the ideas he finds around him. This is why man is at once the molder and the molded, the actor and acted upon of history. We are all a part of an existential situation that is, and yet is not, of our own making. In a very real sense of the word, we are shaped by generations long past, yet have a role to play in the shaping process for generations to come. It is this capacity to choose, limited by the framework we have inherited, which man must come to understand and deal with if he is to be truly "educated."

In principle, therefore, it does not matter whether one generation applauds the previous generation or hisses it— in either event, it carries the previous generation within itself. If the image were not so baroque, we might present the generations not horizontally but vertically, one on top of the other, like acrobats in the circus making a human tower. Rising one on the shoulders of another, he who is on top enjoys the sensation of dominating the rest; but he should also note that at the same time he is the prisoner of the others. This would serve to warn us that what has passed is not merely the past and nothing more, that we are not riding free in the air but standing on its shoulders, that we are in and of the past, a most definite past which continues the human trajectory up to the present moment, which could have been very different from what it was, but which, once having been, is irremediable—it is our present, in which, whether we like it or not, we thrash about like shipwrecked sailors.[5]

---

[5] José Ortega y Gasset, *Man and Crisis,* pp. 53-54.

Unless he seeks only the freedom of shipwrecked sailors, freedom to drown in an existential sea, the individual desperately needs to recognize that his truly liberating capacity to choose is hinged upon a moral framework and certain civilized preconditions which at once limit and enhance his choice. It is this recognition that constitutes civilization.

Civilized Man

What is it then, that civilized man comes to value? One possible answer is given by Harold Gray, the creator of Little Orphan Annie and of the equally delightful Maw Green, Irish washerwoman and homey philosopher *par excellence*. In one of Gray's comic strips, he confronts Maw Green with a slobbering, unkempt, aggressive boob, who shouts, "I got rights, ain't I? I'm as good as any o' those big shots! *Nobody's* better'n *me!* I say all men are *born equal!* Ain't that right?"

Maw Green maintains her boundless good humor and agrees that all men are indeed born equal, but she turns aside to confide to the reader, "But thank Hiven a lot of folks outgrow it!"

Perhaps that civilizing task of "outgrowing it" is how the educative process can best help the individual. Yet in a time of collapsing standards, of "campus revolts," such a task for the educative process seems impossible of fulfillment. If so, Mario Savio and Mark Rudd may be samples of things to come, of tomorrow's torchbearers upon whom our civilization depends.

Surely, such a prospect is frightening to most of us. If

we are to avoid such a fate, the underlying problem must
be faced squarely: Does a proper definition of the nature of
the universe and the nature and role of man within the
universe presuppose the existence of a fixed standard of
value, universally applicable to all men at all times? To
accept such a view is to challenge directly the root assumption of the modern world . . . a world unwilling to accept
the discipline inherent in such a fixed-value system, a world
finding self-congratulation in its illusory man-made heaven
on earth, a heaven blending equal portions of subjectivism
and relativism.

Man Must Be Free to Choose

There have been among us those men of intellect and
integrity who have challenged the dominant mentality of
the age, warning that man must be free to choose and yet
properly instructed in the making of his choice. They have
insisted that proper values can emerge and be defined by
the passage of time and the accumulation of human experience. This accumulated wisdom, this framework of
values, thus provides an enhancement of meaningful choice,
not limiting but rather clarifying the individual's power to
decide. Such individual choice, plus the framework within
which that choice takes place, is a reflection of higher
values than society itself:

> Freedom of the human personality cannot be given by
> society, and by its source and nature it cannot depend
> upon society—it belongs to man himself, as a spiritual
> being. And society, unless it makes totalitarian claims,

can only recognize this freedom. This basic truth about freedom was reflected in the doctrines of natural law, of the rights of man, independent of the state, of freedom, not only as freedom within society, but freedom from society with its limitless claims on man.[6]

To a maverick like Berdyaev, freedom was the key word, but even he admitted that man was a spiritual being and that nature had her own laws demanding respect from the individual as he made his choices.

Many others in the civilized tradition of individual freedom and a fixed moral framework have perceived that the individual must be not only free, but sufficiently educated in the proper values to permit intelligent choice. Albert Jay Nock, for instance, believed that

> . . . the Great Tradition would go on "because the forces of nature are on its side," and it had an invincible ally, "the self-preserving instinct of humanity." Men could forsake it, but come back to it they would. They had to, for their collective existence could not permanently go on without it. Whole societies might deny it, as America had done, substituting bread and buncombe, power and riches or expediency; "but in the end, they will find, as so many societies have already found, that they must return and seek the regenerative power of the Great Tradition, or lapse into decay and death."[7]

Nock was not alone in his insistence upon such standards

---

[6] Nicholas Berdyaev, *The Realm of Spirit and The Realm of Caesar,* pp. 59-60.

[7] Robert M. Crunden, *The Mind & Art of Albert Jay Nock,* p. 134.

for the education of future generations. He stood in the distinguished company of such men as Paul Elmer More, T. S.
Eliot, C. S. Lewis, and Gilbert K. Chesterton, to name but
a few of the defenders of the Great Tradition. These have
been the civilized men of our age.

With Canon Bernard Iddings Bell, the distinguished Epis-
copal clergyman who saw so clearly the tendency of our
times, we might ponder our future:

> I am quite sure that the trouble with us has been that
> we have not seriously and bravely put to ourselves the
> question, "What is man?" or, if and when we have asked
> it, we have usually been content with answers too easy
> and too superficial. Most of us were trained to believe—
> and we have gone on the assumption ever since—that in
> order to be modern and intelligent and scholarly all that
> is required is to avoid asking "Why am I?" and immerse
> oneself in a vast detail of specialized study and in cease-
> less activity. We have been so busy going ahead that we
> have lost any idea of where it is exactly that we are going
> or trying to go. This is, I do believe, the thing that has
> ruined the world in the last half century.[8]

We have lost our philosophic way in the educational
community. We have often forgotten the moral necessity
of freedom, and have usually forgotten the self-discipline
which freedom must reflect if it is to function within the
moral order. As parents, as human beings, as members of
society, we must insist that our educational framework produce neither automatons nor hellions. The individual must

---

[8] Bernard Iddings Bell, *Crisis in Education,* p. 162.

be free to choose, yet must be provided with a framework of values within which meaningful, civilized choice can take place. That twofold lesson must lie at the heart of any renaissance of American education.

3. *Scientism and the Collapse of Standards*

IF THE IDEAL of an educational system is to give children a sense of their individuality and a sense of proper values, the next question arises: "How well is our present educational system fulfilling these fundamental tasks?" The answer is far from encouraging.

Our modern "system" seems bent upon violating freedom (thus denying the concept of the individual) while also violating the framework of values within which the individual exercises his freedom (thus denying the concept of a transcendent reality). True education as we defined it earlier, based upon the individual's freedom to choose and upon a meaningful moral framework within which the individual makes his choices, thus becomes doubly impossible of achievement.

As science and technology have performed their wonders in material achievements, it has been easy to dismiss moral questions (and those who deal with such questions) as unimportant since they apparently do not contribute to "Progress." Such a view has been so largely accepted in our time that the validity of the whole moral framework has been called into question. We seem to have reached a point in our society where science and technology have so advanced our material fortunes that we feel we need look no further for guidance or salvation.

Such scientistic values have played a larger and larger role in our modern educational processes. Let me hasten to draw the distinction between the scientistic and the scientific outlook. Man's pursuit of an improved understanding of his material world is an important and legitimate *scientific* activity, an activity of prime interest to all inquiring minds who have lived on this earth. *Scientism,* the assumption that modern man may now find *all* his values in science to the exclusion of any other guideline, is a totally different concept, a concept peculiar to our materialistic times. One of the men perceiving this tendency was the late Mahatma Gandhi:

> Modern education tends to turn our eyes away from the Spirit. The possibilities of the spirit-force therefore do not appeal to us and our eyes become riveted on the evanescent, transistory and material force.

The modern barbarian produced by such scientistic educational attitudes remains blind to a lesson learned long ago and transmitted from one generation to the next in all civilized communities: The world in which man finds himself can be understood only if he turns at least in part to abstractions that go beyond the merely material. The man who perceives the presence of *only* the material soon finds *himself* indistinguishable from the stones around him.

The Authoritarian Type, Determined to Manipulate Society

As our technological civilization advances further and further in its study of *things* as a substitute for the study of men and their ideas, a new sort of personality comes to occupy the center stage. This new personality sees the entire universe and all its components, individuals included, as portions of a great machine which can be manipulated according to preconceived notions. Men who thus begin to fancy themselves qualified to serve as manipulators of others, men who feel bound by no higher authority, become narrow and bigoted.

Cardinal Newman described such a man in the middle of the last century:

> The various busy world, spread out before our eyes, is physical, but it is more than physical; and, in making its actual system identical with his scientific analysis, such a Professor as I have imagined was betraying a want of a philosophical depth, and an ignorance of what a University Teacher ought to be. He was no longer a teacher of liberal knowledge, but a narrow-minded bigot.

Such bigots are poor judges of what constitutes a decent educational framework. They are likely to assume that man is no more than the final result of the forces acting upon him. This leaves no room for personality, individuality, or free will. Once such a view of the individual is adopted, the idea that men can be manipulated for social goals never lags far behind. Thus, we have a startlingly new concept of education:

Perhaps it is still premature to predict that we will, within the next generation, be able to produce, through drugs or manipulation of the environment, very significant changes in memory and learning capacity of children and even adults. Nonetheless, the current research with mice indicates that such things are theoretically possible, and it is therefore not too early to begin to discuss the social and philosophical problems that such possibilities will generate.[1]

Both the biochemist and the teacher of the future will combine their skills and insights for the educational and intellectual development of the child. Tommy needs a bit more of an immediate memory stimulator; Jack could do with a chemical attention-span stretcher; Rachel needs an anticholinestrase to slow down her mental processes; Joan, some puromycin—she remembers too many details, and gets lost.

To be sure, all our data thus far comes from the brains of goldfish and rodents. But is anyone so certain that the chemistry of the brain of a rat (which, after all, is a fairly complex mammal) is so different from that of the brain of a human being that he dare neglect this challenge—or even gamble—when the stakes are so high?[2]

It seems that man is not to be exempt from the new manipulators. In that same issue of *Saturday Review*, Joseph Wood Krutch reported a speech by a professor of biophysics:

---

[1] Peter Schrag, "Education in America," *Saturday Review*, Jan. 20, 1968, p. 45.

[2] David Krech, "The Chemistry of Learning," *Saturday Review*, Jan. 20, 1968, p. 68.

Robert Sinsheiner, professor of biophysics at Cal Tech, . . . declared before his institution's 75th anniversary conference that the scientist has now in effect become both Nature with a capital N and God with a capital G. Until today, he stated, prophecy has been a very chancy business, but now that science has become "the prime mover of change," it is not unreasonable to hope that the race of prophets employing its methods may have become reliable. Science has now proved beyond question that there is no qualitative difference between the animate and the inanimate, and though we don't yet know exactly how the inanimate becomes conscious, there is every reason to believe that we will soon be rid of that bothersome mystery also. "It has become increasingly clear," Professor Sinsheiner said, "that all the properties of life can be understood to be simply inherent in the material properties of the complex molecule which comprises the cell." Already we make proteins; soon we will make viruses, and then living cells—which will be, as he calls it, "the second Genesis."

What better examples could be given of the scientistic hubris which today dominates so much of our thinking? We are being confronted with Faust's bargain—give up our souls and gain power in return.

Traditionally, education has not been concerned so exclusively with the mere manipulation of the individual. The teacher found himself within a framework of values, within a situation faced in common by all men. To teach, therefore, did not mean to manipulate the young into some "socially acceptable" pattern. Instead, teaching meant sharing with the student the mystery of being human. Today's scientistic approach promises to do away with the human condition entirely, putting its own goals and means in place of the individual human being and his feelings, aspirations, and qualifications. C. S. Lewis has predicted that such a change in our educational and social philosophy is a move toward "the abolition of man."

The Transcendent Order

The story is told that one of our leading physicists concerned with nuclear projects spied a turtle one day while taking a walk with a friend. Thinking he might take it home to his family, he picked it up and carried it with him for a few steps. Suddenly, he stopped, retraced his steps, and, as nearly as possible, replaced the turtle where he had first discovered it.

"Why did you do that?" his friend asked.

The reply: "It just struck me that perhaps, for one man, I have tampered enough with the universe."

It is a sobering thought. There are signs that our power over nature may become uncontrollable. The size, complexity, and uncertainty of the choices available to us might become so great that no one is qualified to make those choices. Could it be that each time we apparently subdue a part of the natural order, we merely cause a dislocation of natural processes which will return to haunt us in a new form? Could it be that our polluted atmosphere and our polluted water are symbols of an ecological equation in which nature herself will have the last laugh? Could it be that man, in his denial of a higher power than science, threatens to destroy himself?

Is it possible that the end result of scientism will be the destruction of all values, including the very human beings who hold those values? Man's search for meaning in his life has always centered on discovery of a higher truth, something even more certain than his existence as an individual. It is the denial of any possible higher reality that finally leads scientism to deny the individual as well. Some modern men have perceived this necessary connection between the identity of the individual and the existence of a higher reality. One such flash of insight was granted to the playwright, Eugene O'Neill:

> Most modern plays are concerned with the relation between man and man, but that does not interest me at all. I am interested only in the relation between man and God. Anyone trying to do big work nowadays must have this big subject behind all the little subjects, or he is simply scribbling around on the surface of things.

We have been "scribbling around on the surface of things" and wondering what was happening to our civilization. We have been trying to get along without God and attempting to put society, scientism, and political manipulation in his place. We may yet discover that despite television, air conditioning, and all the other trappings of modern material civilization, man cannot survive such self-idolatry. In our attempt, we are, in George Schuyler's phrase, "like a colony of ants riding on the end of a log floating down the Mississippi, while discussing destiny."

If we have no values to transmit to our young, we need not be surprised that we live in an increasingly valueless age.

The Academy and the Collapse of Values

Nowhere is the collapse of values which plagues our educational community and our society more apparent than in the academy. That we live in an age of tremendous activity may be but a sign of decay. As Ortega y Gasset has commented, "In the world today a great thing is dying; it is truth. Without a certain margin of tranquillity, truth succumbs."

Perhaps the reason for all the "sound and fury, signifying nothing" is that somehow we have lost our common sense and substituted a total intellectual anarchy in its place. Man has never been more problematic to himself than in modern times. We no longer seem to know what we are; and the growing body of scientific thought engaged in the study of man seems to do far more to confuse than to clarify the problem for us. Never have we possessed more facts, but never have we suffered such a poverty of insight into the human condition. Thus, we seem to run faster and faster in pursuit of a progressively more illusive truth. Indeed, many people have given up the search entirely, and today regard truth and the meaning of life as "metaphysical" concepts, insisting that really "significant" scientific investigation must center on the mere gathering of information.

And what information we have been gathering! The isolation produced by the jargon of the various disciplines, each busy gathering facts quite apart from any higher standard of truth, has often rendered the work of these specialists unintelligible to one another or to the society of which they are a part. Indeed, any unified view of culture is totally unattainable for the modern scientistic mentality. Unity implies standards; standards imply a scale of values which can be universally applied. When scientism promises to provide us with constantly new "facts," supposedly implying a constantly changing world view, such an empirical paradise can hardly accommodate itself to immutable values. Finally, the fact chasers must reject the concept of value altogether.

Those who would abandon all the old standards of good, those who would condition the human race to accept their new system, are faced with a terrible dilemma. If the conditioners have no fixed standards of their own, what standards can they inculcate in the human raw material they control? The blind are leading the blind.

If we can indeed "see through" first principles, if we can "see through" everything and anything, then everything and anything must be transparent. C. S. Lewis has reminded us that a wholly transparent world is an invisible world, and to "see through" all things is finally the same as not to see at all.

A patron saint of the intellectual climate of twentieth century America was J. Allen Smith (originator of the "debunking" view of the Founding Fathers and the United States Constitution, later made famous by Charles Beard's *An Economic Interpretation of the Constitution*). Smith, in a moment of reflection, apparently had misgivings about the course of events: "The trouble with us reformers is that we made reform a crusade against standards. Well, we smashed them all, and now neither we nor anyone else have anything left."

Nothing left! Strong words, coming from a prophet of the modern academy. If Smith was right, if standards are all smashed, then to what can we turn in educating our young people?

What Is the Truth?

This failure of standards within the modern academy can be easily demonstrated. One of the foremost students of St. Thomas Aquinas, Professor Josef Pieper, gives graphic illustration:

> The medieval philosophers, in studying Aristotle and Plato, wished to know all those things and only those things which were true. Where the truths of these philosophers were not complete, they asked themselves how to complete them.
>
> There is an enormous difference between this attitude and that usually held nowadays and which we consider the sole possible and responsible attitude toward "sources." For the student especially, that difference is of vital importance. Anyone who asks Thomas his opinion receives a reply which makes perfectly clear what he, Thomas, considers to be the truth—even when his reply is couched in the form of a quotation from Aristotle. But if we are asked our opinion, we reply with historically documented quotations which may reveal a good many

things—for example, how widely read we are—but fail
to reveal one thing alone; what we ourselves hold to be
the truth.[3]

Such a tendency is painfully apparent in modern philosophy. One of the latest "isms" to catch the fancy of modern
philosophers is structuralism. Dr. Michel Foucault, for example, insists that each thinker can be no more than the
point of condensation and articulation of the total thought
structure, within which he finds his place. The philosopher,
then, can possess no original insight into the nature of things.
Instead, he reclassifies thoughts and words according to the
thought processes within his civilization. It is this total
social process which gives man his structure. For the structuralist, man without this social structure would be "a mere
figure in the sand whose forms are washed away by the sea."

Such totally valueless thought processes are increasingly
typical of the age in which we live. Indeed, we might ask
the structuralists one question. If a philosopher's insight is
no more than a series of essentially meaningless shufflings
and reshufflings of previous words and values, why should
the thinking of the structuralist himself present any exception to the rule? But to deal in these terms is to play their
game, admitting that all is ultimately pointless and meaningless and without direction. Our very conversation with one
another comes to mean less and less until it finally means
nothing. Ortega quotes a seventeenth century satirist who
put his finger squarely on the final results of such thinking:

---

[3] Josef Pieper, *Guide to Thomas Aquinas*, p. 52.

The Creator made everything out of nothing,
This one [man] nothing out of everything, and in
   conclusion,
The one made the world and the other has destroyed it.

An Age Without Roots

How, then, shall we characterize our age?

Our age is characterized by the strange presumption
that it is superior to all past time; more than that, by its
leaving out of consideration all that is past, by recognizing no classical or normative epochs, by looking on
itself as a new life superior to all previous forms and ir-
reducible to them. I doubt if our age can be understood
without keeping firm hold on this observation, for that
is precisely its special problem. If it felt that it was decadent, it would look on other ages as superior to itself,
which would be equivalent to esteeming and admiring
them and venerating the principles by which they were
inspired. Our age would then have clear and firmly held
ideals, even if incapable of realizing them. But the truth
is exactly the contrary; we live at a time when man believes himself fabulously capable of creation, but he does
not know what to create. Lord of all things, he is not lord
of himself. He feels lost amid his own abundance. With
more means at its disposal, more knowledge, more tech-
nique than ever, it turns out that the world to-day goes
the same way as the worst of worlds that have been; it
simply drifts.[4]

---

[4] José Ortega y Gasset, *The Revolt of the Masses,* (Norton, 1957),
p. 44.

Thus, the world drifts, without a moral code. It is not that we have exchanged an antiquated previous code for a bright new mode of behavior. Instead, modern man aspires to live without *any* moral code. Much of the talk about the "new morality" is better characterized as a departure from any moral standard whatsoever. More precisely, it might be defined as the desire to call the old immorality the new morality. We are not contrasting a rising new civilization with the declining old one, a rising new standard replacing a dying code. In Ortega's words: "If you are unwilling to submit to any norm, you have . . . to submit to the norm of denying all morality, and this is not amoral, but immoral. It is a negative morality which preserves the empty form of the other."[5]

C. E. M. Joad suggests that the principal characteristics of a society without moral standards are "luxury, scepticism, weariness, and superstition." He adds that another sure sign of a decadent society is an individual preoccupation with self and a totally subjectivist view of the world and all higher values. Once the individual comes to believe that he may think whatever he likes with equal validity, that any value is no better or worse than any other value, then the decadent society must indeed be at hand.

Such a society, of course, will allow no limitation upon individual sexual mores, and will also undercut other traditional patterns of action. This is readily observable in our own society in the decline in genuine individual charity, mercy, pity, honesty, and unselfishness. We live in an age

---

[5] *Ibid.,* p. 189.

which has not so much rejected these values as it has simply refused to bother to think about the subject at all. We are becoming, in the truest possible sense of the word, an age without standards.

Art and the Modern World

While it is true that most critics and many minor scribblers are true sons of our present society, it is also true that Henry James, T. S. Eliot, Ezra Pound, Thomas Mann, Marcel Proust, and the other major literary figures of our time have consistently devoted their art to a bitter rejection of the modern spirit. It seems that meaningful literary production can only arise in those who possess some value system, who reject the flaccid and valueless spirit of the age. Never have we had more novelists and poets . . . never have there been fewer great novels and great poems.

Meanwhile, what sort of art has been produced? Work filled largely with hate, hate directed not merely at individuals but at an entire universe which must be hated simply because it is meaningless.

Coupled with this hatred of all men and all things, so-called "artistic freedom" has released a flood of sexuality, violence, and perversion without a peer in man's recorded history. Joseph Wood Krutch has commented on a list of one hundred books representing this modern tendency that while the list "does include certain works which are neither beatnik, sadistic, existential, nor sexually perverse, at least half—and perhaps two-thirds—of them might, I think, be classified as guideposts to perdition."

What, it might be asked, has all this to do with education? Even granted that scientism had stripped us of all values and that this is reflected in our philosophy and our art, what possible connection does this have with what our children are learning in school? Unfortunately, the connection is painfully direct. Before we can begin to discuss the improvement of individuals and of the society which they compose, we must first of all grasp the fact that there *is* a difference between the good and the bad.

> If the object of education is the improvement of men, then any system of education that is without values is a contradiction in terms. A system that seeks bad values is bad. A system that denies the existence of values denies the possibility of education. Relativism, scientism, skepticism, and anti-intellectualism, the four horsemen of the philosophical apocalypse, have produced that chaos in education which will end in the disintegration of the West.[6]

Our national prosperity, the welfare of our institutions, and the welfare of all individuals depend directly upon the values which we inculcate in our educational system. If we deny to our children the philosophical framework of values by which they may order their conduct, we are denying them a true education and guaranteeing the decline of our civilization. There are other dimensions to our problem, but this matter of the rejection of value is of prime importance

---

[6] Robert M. Hutchins, *The Conflict in Education in a Democratic Society,* pp. 71-72.

in fully appreciating the sad estate unto which we have fallen.

One hard-headed Yankee who perceived the proper place of moral values and the close connection between self-restraint and freedom was Ralph Waldo Emerson:

All our political disasters grow as logically out of our attempts in the past to do without justice, as the sinking of some part of your house comes of defect in the foundation. One thing is plain; a certain personal virtue is essential to freedom; and it begins to be doubtful whether our corruption in this country has not gone a little over the mark of safety, so that when canvassed we shall be found to be made up of a majority of reckless self-seekers. The divine knowledge has ebbed out of us and we do not know enough to be free.

4. The Decline of Intellect

THE LOWERED ETHICAL STANDARDS of our age have been matched by a decline of intellect. Today, we place progressively less faith in man's intellectual powers, substituting a faith in institutionalized arrangements and methods. If we would help our young to develop and implement proper values in their lives, we must first recover the intellectual integrity to distinguish between good and bad. Such intellectual integrity rests upon a firm belief that man *can* think, and that no genuine substitute exists for human thought. If the school is to transmit the intellectual and cultural heritage, and develop in students a proper sense of morality, it must begin by teaching them to think.

Conversely, if we would help our young people to think, we must provide a cultural and moral framework within which their intellectual capacities may be exercised. Yet, this disciplined thought is precisely what is lacking in the home and the school.

Within the existing educational framework, moral and philosophic questions tend to be handled with the neutrality of "scientific objectivity." As the result, our children are provided no philosophic basis for their own thinking. Instead, they take on the protective coloration of the dominant social mores—a form of "social adjustment" which places a premium upon nonthinking. Small wonder that our age of shrinking values also becomes the age of shrinking intellect.

It is not quite fair to say that today's intellectual leaders have no values. Although they are extremely skeptical about values and emphasize that skepticism in all their works, many modern "intellectuals" *do* have their own underlying value system which C. S. Lewis has sharply called into question:

It is an outrage that they should be commonly spoken of as Intellectuals. This gives them the chance to say that he who attacks them attacks Intelligence. It is not so. They are not distinguished from other men by any unusual skill in finding truth nor any virginal ardour to pursue her. Indeed it would be strange if they were: a preserving devotion to truth, a nice sense of intellectual honour, cannot be long maintained without the aid of a sentiment which . . . [they] could debunk as easily as any other. It is not excess of thought but defect of fertile and generous emotion that marks them out. Their heads are no bigger than the ordinary: it is the atrophy of the chest beneath that makes them seem so.

And all the time—such is the tragi-comedy of our situation—we continue to clamour for those very qualities we are rendering impossible. You can hardly open a periodical without coming across the statement that what our civilization needs is more "drive," or dynamism, or self-sacrifice, or "creativity." In a sort of ghastly simplicity we remove the organ and demand the function. We make men without chests and expect of them virtue and enterprise. We laugh at honour and are shocked to find traitors in our midst. We castrate and bid the geldings be fruitful.[1]

"There Is No Truth"

What are some of the philosophic underpinnings of the educational system now reaping such a bitter harvest? One of the most basic principles of the Deweyite pragmatism and instrumentalism which infects our schools and our social order is that the truth of an idea is measurable only by the consequences to which it leads. If the consequences of an idea are good, then the proposition is true. How do we measure good consequences? The good, so we are told by the instrumentalists, is that which achieves the proper social ends.

Does the individual have judgment in this matter? Is there some divine sanction by which we can evaluate such ends? The modern answer to both questions is "No." The measure of good is now exclusively social, eliminating individual judgment, eliminating any fixed standard of right and wrong, and indeed eliminating the very concept of truth.

The fact that a modern intellectual no longer searches for truth should not be construed to mean that he no longer searches for knowledge. The distinction comes in the fact that his search for knowledge evidences no interest in any

---

[1] C. S. Lewis, *The Abolition of Man*, pp. 34-35.

ultimate reality beyond the immediate workability of an idea. Any value without direct application to the here and the now is considered pointless and unworthy of transmission as "knowledge."

Most men who have lived in Western civilization have premised their thinking upon the presence of a higher reality, dimly perceived yet serving as the basis for all human endeavor. That human endeavor was an attempt to discover and live in consonance with that higher reality through the use of man's *unique* capacity to reason. The modern intellectual, applying "scientific" methods and standards to his investigation, finds no evidence of such a higher reality or any higher side of man as reflected in the individual. Thus, man comes to be viewed as nothing more than a creature engaged in the process of adaptation to his environment, a creature possessing neither soul nor mind in the sense in which Western man has developed the concept. The intellect itself, the individual's very capacity to think, is finally called into question.

Today's educational framework affords no place for the mind. The concept of mind always demanded discipline on the part of the individual if the fruits of his intellectual processes were to command the attention and respect of his fellows. But in today's denial of mind, the new keys to man's personality are assumed to be composed exclusively of emotional factors, psychological "adjustment," and materialistic creature necessities.

"Adjust to your environment," our young people are constantly told. Such a denial of intellect has the effect of lowering standards for society as a whole while robbing each of us of the essence of his individuality.

Thought, if granted any validity at all, has come to be regarded as a rather mechanical process, measurable, and computable.

The social engineers predict that such intellectual concentrations will be beneficial to mankind as a whole and to each individual as well. The idea advanced by Julian Huxley of a "thought bank" is considered by them in all seriousness. To an inquiry of *The New York Times* in 1958, one of the scientists consulted about the socio-intellectual aspects of the year 2000, Professor John Weir of California Institute of Technology, answered that there will be no conflict among the thinking of individuals because "a common Thought Bank will be established from which all will receive instructions and to which all may repair in case of doubt." Less "scientific" but equally enthusiastic for a society that will have eliminated "divisiveness," are the recommendations of Professor Robert C. Angell. In *Free Society and Moral Crisis*, the author identifies what he calls the "moral web" with socialized attitudes, and "moral crisis" with deviant behavior. It is incidental to our present argument that Mr. Angell never tells us how one distinguishes whether a "deviant" group is *good or bad*—how one tells a saint from a delinquent, a gang from the twelve apostles—when both disrupt the social fabric and neither behaves according to "the common values of their culture." What is, however, relevant here is that the remedies he suggests for "social and moral integration" are all collectivistic measures, reached through public discussions in high schools, television panels, Boy Scout and YMCA programs, group therapy, prisoner rehabilitation, and so on.[2]

Forget and Adjust

Such attitudes rest on two suppositions: 1. All past thinking and moral judgment must be discounted if not dismissed since it predates the definition of truth as "social good"; and 2. The preparation for those living in such a society must no longer aim toward the education of a freely choosing moral agent but instead must emphasize the "adjustment" of the individual to the total social good.

. . . the difference between the old and the new education will be an important one. Where the old initiated, the new merely "conditions." The old dealt with its pupils as grown birds deal with young birds when they teach them to fly: the new deals with them more as the poultry-keeper deals with young birds—making them thus or thus for purposes of which the birds know nothing. In a word, the old was a kind of propagation—men transmitting manhood to men: the new is merely propaganda.[3]

Such an educational system is not designed to develop a capacity for thinking or to halt the decline of intellect.

It may well be that such an attempt at placing society over the individual (and, indeed, over God as well), would be unacceptable to many persons now living in this nation or in the Western world. It is true, however, that these are the dominant ideas among intellectuals who will largely

---

[2] Thomas Molnar, *The Decline of the Intellectual,* pp. 219-220.

[3] Lewis, *op. cit.,* pp. 32-33.

influence generations to come. The departure from tradition, morality, and even human thought which seems far advanced in theory, has scarcely begun in practice. The most sweeping changes in our society lie ahead unless we decide to reverse the process.

In facing that decision, let us compare the new values with the traditional, with our Western heritage of discovery and development in morality, science, law, and art, a heritage based upon a firm and unswerving faith in man's ability to reason, in his unique gift of intellect. Remove man's power to think and to act on the basis of his thinking and you have destroyed the very quality which makes him human. To abandon such a history is to create a vacuum quite likely to be filled with the new "philosophy of change."

The Philosophy of Change

Today, we are told that we have swept aside the dead hand of the past with its constricting and confining tradition and morality. We are told that the disciplines of former ages no longer bind us. We are told that, in view of these rapid transformations, all standards are relative to social considerations; man and society are whatever we choose to make of them. Thus, change itself, change for its own sake, becomes the dominant philosophy of the age. A variety of experiences (no matter what their quality) with constant growth (no matter in what direction) and constant activity (no matter how frenzied) are now to serve as a suitable educational goal. Here again, the decline of intellect is most graphically demonstrated.

What are the standards for judging the purposes and values thus successively emerging in the pupil's mind? If the teacher himself has no general aim, nor final values to which all this process is related; if education itself is to grow "in whatever direction a novelly emerging future renders most feasible. . . ."[4]

This is a pointless procession of the blind leading the blind. An "educated" man is often regarded as one who is quick and clever in discussion and ready and willing to discuss anything. To discuss freely on all sides of all questions, without standards, without values, is to insure the creation of a generation of uninformed and talkative minds, a living demonstration of the decline of intellect.

During Goethe's travels in Italy, he spent some time in the company of an Italian captain. Describing the man, Goethe remarked, "This captain is a true representative of many of his compatriots. Here is a particularly typical trait of his. As I would often remain silent and thoughtful, he said to me once: 'What are you thinking about? One ought never to think, thinking ages one! One should never confine oneself to one single thing because he then goes mad: *he needs to have a thousand things, a confusion in his head.'*"[5]

The New Age of Doubt

How different is modern education from that traditionally followed in Western civilization! St. Thomas always warned students never to leave any difficulty unresolved in their

---

4 Jacques Maritain, *Education at the Crossroads*, p. 17.
5 José Ortega y Gasset, *Meditations*, p. 81.

study, to always fully understand whatever they read or heard and to "avoid speechifying on anything whatsoever." How few modern students follow such an injunction! He also warned teachers that they must "never dig a ditch [in front of the student] that you fail to fill up."[6]

St. Thomas well knew that cleverly to raise doubts, forever to seek and never find, was, when carried to the extreme, the great enemy of both education and thought.

Many modern teachers have not learned what St. Thomas knew so well. We live in an age in which we are kept busy by endless induction. Today we substitute facts for truths. We engage in a constant round of activity on the assumption that, in Richard Weaver's caustic phrase, "experience will tell us what we are experiencing." No standards, no evaluation, no genuine thought—it is to such a nightmare that the concept of change finally leads us. And traditional philosophy is dismissed by modern man as "static." Thus, any values not constantly shifting are regarded as old hat, as unworthy for a "modern" mind. Institutions, values, attitudes that show constancy are finally dismissed by a philosophy of ceaseless change.

At any given moment, so says this new philosophy, the only means by which society can properly determine what values are acceptable is through a temporary consensus. Thus, we find a constant flight of endlessly shifting ideas and values, somehow to be caught on the wing and rendered intelligible at a particular moment in time. Society now becomes the final arbiter of a "truth" as changing as the sum-

---

[6] Maritain, *op. cit.,* p. 50.

mer breeze, thus necessitating endless reratification by society. It should be clear that the only constant in such a society would be this supposedly infallible method of arriving at the truth.

The main concern of our modern intellectuals has been, not the discovery of an enduring reality, but rather the mastery of a method for measuring change. We no longer measure growth toward an ideal, simply because no ideal remains. When there is no longer a standard by which to test it, the intellect is clearly in decline.

The collapse of standards and of the intellect is closely allied to the rise in scientism, as discussed earlier. Modern naturalism, materialism, and scientism hold that only material, physically measurable quantities and values can exist. Thus, all other standards of religion, ethics, and culture, including any accomplishment of the mind, are swept aside. The result is an intellectual and moral vacuum.

This vacuum extends to the most minor and everyday concerns of curriculum. Traditional subjects are being displaced by courses in art appreciation, fly-casting, and other intellectual activities equally insignificant.

A value system is essential if students are to sort out and make use of the vast assortment of miscellaneous "facts" thrust upon them. Some hierarchy of values is essential to the use of the mind or intellect. And it is not surprising that young people who have thus been "educated" to deny their uniqueness, their capacity to think, should feel unfulfilled and confused by the world around them.

Meanwhile, the trend continues toward a collective mentality. Under a theory of ceaseless change and total "social goals," all values are determined by the current state of the environment. The environment, subject to manipulation by the state, may be depended upon to breed conditions demanding ever larger involvement of government in society. State control of society and education can be depended upon to provide systematic indoctrination through the innumerable channels of propaganda opened by the decline of intellect.

Social Failure

Such a system of total control, supposedly relieving the individual of all responsibility and all concerns, must prove fatal in the end.

Youthful enthusiasm and the joy of living may conceal the inner vacuum for some time, at least until one goes through the initial stages of adulthood—settling down in a trade or profession, getting married, having children, and finding a place in society. But in the midstream of life just before age makes its first appearance, the existential questions about the meaning of life as it concerns the individual are inevitably asked. Then the haphazard, practical cleverness picked up in the school and along the way proves frighteningly inadequate.[7]

Thus, there comes to the individual something of the dichotomy suffered by society: the simultaneous sense of power and insecurity. Today, we are told that everything is possible for us. We are taught to believe this; yet, never

---

[7] Thomas Molnar, *The Future of Education,* pp. 87-88.

has talk of a returning barbarism and decay been more widespread throughout Western civilization. We bury ourselves under every conceivable material and political "security," only to find ourselves increasingly insecure and unprepared for what tomorrow may bring.

We may embrace the pragmatic idea that circumstances will decide the truth. But Ortega has reminded us that it is not circumstances which finally decide, but our character. We can move the choice away from the individual to mass man and society as a whole, we can abandon all of our traditional values in a wave of ceaseless change; still, somewhere deep in our hearts we know that *we* are deciding. We know this, even when our very indecision finally forms the future. Choice is not so easily abandoned.

Choice becomes increasingly difficult when our educational system turns out men capable of running the technical machinery of civilization but totally ignorant of the principles upon which that civilization rests.

Civilisation is not "just there," it is not self-supporting. It is artificial and requires the artist or the artisan. If you want to make use of the advantages of civilisation, but are not prepared to concern yourself with the upholding of civilisation—you are done. In a trice you find yourself left without civilisation. Just a slip, and when you look around everything has vanished into air. The primitive forest appears in its native state, just as if curtains covering pure Nature had been drawn back. The jungle is always primitive and, vice versa, everything primitive is mere jungle.[8]

---

[8] José Ortega y Gasset, *The Revolt of the Masses,* p. 88.

Yes, the jungle is always there; and when a society begins to insist that there are no lasting values, that the individual is incompetent to choose his own path or to think his own thoughts, then the civilization based upon fixed moral values and free individual choice is destined to revert to that jungle.

The jungle is close indeed when we believe that a man is no more than the sum of his heredity and environment, and that his behavior, instead of his own choosing, is molded for him by his surroundings. A man thus molded could not be responsible for his action. A society composed of such men would be an irresponsible society that seeks wages without work, pleasure without pain, and learning without effort.

Today, we often fail to see any relationship between crime and punishment, between effort and reward; we have no understanding of a hierarchy of values, no concept of a total unity governing human existence. The predictable result: a nation of spoiled children. These spoiled children are of all ages, but they share a common conviction that if their insatiable appetites are unsatisfied, someone is being mean to them. This may explain why the promises of science are so uncritically accepted at face value—the fulfillment of all desire in a flood of material goods and scientific progress. We are led to believe that the very riddle of life and death is about to be solved by science. If man can have both eternal life and satiation of all desire in the here and now, then what other god need he worship?

It is true that the price is high; we must be willing to give up our individual capacity to think and to choose, we must be willing to give up any fixed moral code. But what need has man for such things in social paradise?

Individuals within our society become steadily less productive on the intellectual and moral diet they receive. Tocqueville caught the essence of the underlying problem:

> In ages of faith, the final end of life is placed beyond life. The men of those ages, therefore, naturally and almost involuntarily accustom themselves to fix their gaze for many years on some immovable object toward which they are constantly tending; and they learn by insensible degrees to repress a multitude of petty passing desires in order to be the better able to content that great and lasting desire which possesses them. . . . This explains why religious nations have often achieved such lasting results; for whilst they were thinking only of the other world, they had found out the great secret of success in this.[9]

Perhaps the great religious teachers were right after all in their insistence that man must recognize some higher will than his own. Nowhere is this recognition of a higher will more important than in intellectual matters. It would appear that in the modern world all too many men have so exalted the product of their own minds that they have come to see themselves as self-sufficient. In that illusory self-sufficiency, man has come, as we have seen, finally to lose the direction and point of his own intelligence. Indeed, modern man has ceased to believe in the quality of his own individual intellect, and thus brought about one of the fundamental failures of our age: the decline of intellect.

---

[9] Richard Weaver, *Ideas Have Consequences,* p. 118.

5. *Discipline or Disaster?*

MODERN MAN'S COLLAPSE of values and intellectual decline must be attributed at least in part to his undisciplined nature. In no other age have men seemed so unwilling to exercise or accept any restraint upon individual appetite. We no longer seem to know how to discipline our young, perhaps because we no longer know how to discipline ourselves. If we could uncover the philosophic underpinnings of this nondiscipline, much of what is happening today in our educational structure would perhaps become more understandable—and less acceptable.

Schools, of course, are not solely to blame for the collapse of values and discipline in our society. Yet, at a time when individuals cry out for spiritual meaning and direction in their lives, all too many of our schools seem to play down the role of discipline, pinning their hopes upon more elaborate physical facilities, more of the "self-expression" and "recreation" that already reflect the undisciplined values of our age.

If we fail to sow the seeds of values and of discipline among our young, we should not be surprised at the harvest. As Albert Jay Nock phrased it in *The Theory of Education in the United States:*

Nature takes her own time, sometimes a long time, about exacting her penalty—but exact it in the end she always does, and to the last penny. It would appear, then, that a society which takes no account of the educable person, makes no place for him, does nothing with him, is taking a considerable risk; so considerable that in the whole course of human experience, as far as our records go, no society ever yet has taken it without coming to great disaster.

To educate the young in proper values and proper self-discipline is not unduly complicated. Children have no stronger urge than to be "grown up," and are quick to imitate the adult behavior they see around them. The inculcation of proper values and proper self-discipline requires that we act as we wish our children to act. If we would discipline our children, we begin by disciplining ourselves.

But, here is the problem: How can we expect the exercise of self-discipline by parents who are themselves products of a permissive educational system? The sound idea that a child's interests should be taken into account in planning an educational program has been twisted to mean that a child should be given whatever he wants. Parents first abandon to the schools the responsibility for teaching values and discipline; the schools in turn reply that discipline and value-education can best be left to the children themselves. Small wonder that children rebel when thus abandoned by their elders.

Much of the revolt against authority came in the wake of World War I. The 1920's saw the crystallization of an attitude which totally rejected any standard outside the self. Freudian psychologists insisted that restraint of any natural desire is bad. The "new era" theorists taught us that art was the unplanned result of a head-on collision between the artist's personality and the medium of his work. The professional educationists made the cycle complete in telling us that our young should do only what they wish to do. Such evidences of antidiscipline, in psychology, in art, and above all, in education, are now so commonplace that we take them for granted. All of this has gone hand in hand with the subjugation of intellect to emotion, impulse, and instinct.

Freedom Becomes License

A certain balance of freedom and order is essential, not only in education but in all human endeavor. The importance of freedom in the educational process has already been discussed at length. But the peculiar conception of "freedom from" rather than "freedom for" carries with it a rejection of all the values and inner disciplines which are necessary to give freedom any real meaning. Today "freedom" has a quality tending suspiciously toward what an earlier generation would have called "license." "Do what you want when you want to do it," modern society tells its young, and then is surprised when the young do just that!

One of the ultimate contrasts that presents itself in a subject of this kind is that between habit as conceived by Aristotle and nature as conceived by Rousseau.

The first great grievance of the critical humanist

against Rousseau is that he set out to be the individualist
and at the same time attacked analysis, which is indis-
pensable if one is to be a sound individualist. The second
great grievance of the humanist is that Rousseau sought
to discredit habit which is necessary if right analysis is to
be made effective. "The only habit the child should be
allowed to form," says Rousseau, "is that of forming no
habit." How else is the child to follow his bent or genius
and so arrive at full self-expression? The point I am bring-
ing up is of the utmost gravity, for Rousseau is by common consent the father of modern education. To eliminate
from education the idea of a progressive adjustment to a
human law, quite apart from temperament, may be to im-
peril civilization itself. For civilization (another word
that is sadly in need of Socratic defining) may be found
to consist above all in an orderly transmission of right
habits; and the chief agency for securing such a transmission must always be education, by which I mean far
more of course than mere schooling.[1]

Babbitt was right, of course; learning is rapidly declining
in most of our schools, through a steady erosion of standards,
intellect, and discipline. The late President Eliot of Harvard
epitomized the tendency of our time when he insisted, "A
well-instructed youth of eighteen can select for himself a
better course of study than any college faculty, or any wise
man who does not know his ancestors and his previous life,
can possibly select for him. . . . Every youth of eighteen is
an infinitely complex organization, the duplicate of which

---

[1] Irving Babbitt, *Rousseau and Romanticism*, p. 292.

neither does nor ever will exist." The libertarian, of course, centers his case upon the individual, upon a personality whose very uniqueness necessitates freedom of choice; but the libertarians must also help to provide a proper value structure within which that choice takes place, else the choice itself becomes meaningless. It is such a meaningless choice to which President Eliot and most modern education-ists have condemned our young people. In Irving Babbitt's phrase, "The wisdom of all the ages is to be as naught com-pared with the inclination of a sophomore."

Underlying this willingness to allow the young person to pick and choose without discipline or direction is the tacit assumption that no body of knowledge exists as a proper ex-planation of the human condition. The great point becomes not to teach knowledge, but to teach students. If no stan-dards exist, how can they be passed on to the young?

Simply, it may be called the philosophy of "doing what comes naturally." At the intellectual level, for example, it is held that there is some magic value in the uninhibited and uninformed opinion if freely expressed. And so dis-cussion groups are held in the grade schools and the high schools on such subjects as "What do *you* think about the atom bomb?" or "teen-age morality" or "banning *Lady Chatterley's Lover*" or "implementing freedom among un-derprivileged nations" or what not. The poor little dears have scarcely a fact to use as ballast. But no matter. The cult of sensibility believes that continuing, free, unin-hibited discussion will ultimately release the inherent goodness of natural instincts and impulses. The fad for "brainstorming" has passed, but not the philosophy behind it.[2]

Today it seems to be assumed that any opinion whatsoever is justified so long as it is held with sufficient sincerity and emotional fervor. One shares with Irving Babbitt the feeling that "perhaps the best examples of sincerity in this sense are to be found in insane asylums."

In part, this endless capacity for "dialogue" and "the open mind" stems from the same philosophic roots producing our decline of standards and decline of intellect. Unless the individual finally uses that openmindedness as a preparation for the final act of *judgment* and *selection,* that is, uses his free inquiry and fact gathering as a means of finally *reaching a conclusion,* then openmindedness becomes only the drafty, valueless cavern through which blow the cold winds of decline and death.

A society unwilling to discipline its thinking and its young is a society doomed to extinction.

The Education of Leaders

Good or bad leaders will always be with us, and no amount of Rousseau's "General Will" or democratic faith in numerical majorities can change that fact. We will be no better than the quality of the leaders within our society, and the quality of leadership in a democracy will be no higher than the level of popular understanding permits.

_____

[2] Calvin D. Linton, "Higher Education: The Solution—or Part of the Problem?" *Christianity Today,* Feb. 16, 1968.

Unfortunately, a low level of understanding is foredoomed in a society lacking a disciplined educational structure.

We seem unwilling to accept the discipline of genuine language study. Many future voters cannot tell the meaning of such words as grammar, logic, or rhetoric, much less use or appreciate the skills involved. The study of history has fared little better. Through modern "social studies," the sobering truth of history has been carefully concealed from our young. Man's achievements *and* his failures, the painful reality of the fate awaiting the self-indulgent individual, have been carefully buried in reams of uninformed nonsense centering on "group dynamics" or misinformed propaganda slanting the student toward collectivism as a means of solving all our "social problems."

All too many of the subjects taught to America's young people reflect this headlong flight from any meaningful discipline of the mind. A society which thus educates its leaders may expect rough sledding ahead.

The lack of discipline noted in our educational institutions stems from both external and internal weaknesses. Many modern educators cannot control or properly direct their students, nor can they display the internal discipline of mind and heart to control their own intellectual and spiritual behavior. Small wonder that those teachers who are themselves undisciplined prove such poor examples to the young.

Genuine creative capacity involves more than the natural talent of a child. A properly disciplined atmosphere must surround the child to allow his creative capacities to come to light. Children cannot be creative in a vacuum, but a vacuum is exactly what we provide when our teachers are drawn from a philosophic system denying standards and discipline. One of the last century's great commentators on education, Matthew Arnold, once remarked:

> It is . . . sufficiently clear that the teacher to whom you give only a drudge's training, will do only a drudge's work, and will do it in a drudge's spirit: that in order to ensure good instruction even within narrow limits in a school, you must provide it with a master far superior to his scholars.[3]

It should go without saying that a vast number of America's teachers are anything but drudges; many of them show great self-discipline and high standards, which they constantly reflect in the educational experience they are attempting to impart to our young people. Even so, we find far too many teachers of the other sort, lacking discipline and lacking standards. Moreover, even our best teachers are severely handicapped by an educational structure whose underlying philosophy minimizes proper discipline. Many proponents of progressive education insist that learning be set aside in favor of the unreflective and spontaneous desires and attitudes of the child. The child is to be encouraged to follow his own desires in what he studies. Intellectual effort is to be displaced by spontaneous "activity." Competition and a disciplined system of grading are to be shunned,

---

[3] G. H. Bantock, *Freedom and Authority in Education,* p. 98.

since they imply superiority and inferiority. The child is assumed to be able to meet his own educational needs without external pressures. In a word, we are to achieve education without discipline.

A Line of Least Resistance

True education, of course, implies discipline. The discipline of competition, the discipline of standards, the discipline of responsible adults who have determined what is of real and enduring purpose, the discipline of concentration, these are among the essentials of true education. Anything less soon leads to what Irving Babbitt described as a typical result of the "new approach" to learning:

> Having provided such a rich and costly banquet of electives to satisfy the "infinite variety" of youths of eighteen, President Eliot must be somewhat disappointed to see how nearly all these youths insist on flocking into a few large courses; and especially disappointed that many of them should take advantage of the elective system not to work strenuously along the line of their special interests, but rather to lounge through their college course along the line of least resistance.[4]

The new motto in education all too often seems to be "jack of all ideas, master of none" apparently implying that, if our young people dabble in enough subjects, never mind whether they ever master any particular subject, "education" will somehow have taken place. Genuine enlargement of the

---

[4] Irving Babbitt, *Literature and the American College,* p. 35.

mind presupposes sufficiently disciplined study to achieve a grasp of a subject. This must be coupled with the equally necessary discipline of viewing all subjects as portions of a single reality expressive of human existence. An educational philosophy which never allows the student to master any particular subject and which denies the existence of universally applicable general principles is a system calculated to retard the mental growth of its pupils. We have become so concerned about providing "real life situations" in the classroom, so concerned about providing a cultural potpourri based on technological developments in radio, the movies, and television, that the young people educated in our system are no longer in touch with reality, very uncertain as to just who and why they are.

When no inviolable standards remain, it is natural that the teacher will no longer think of himself as being in authority. All discipline must go, since the teacher has no concepts to impart and is to function only as a leader, synchronizing the amorphous collective development of his participants. Thus, external discipline joins internal discipline in the discard. In such a system, one of the keys for genuine education is lost. The relationship between the master and the pupil, between the one who has achieved discipline and the one who has yet to achieve it, ceases to exist. Also lost is much of the traditional authority and prestige of the teacher.

The child-centered school may be attractive to the child, and no doubt is useful as a place in which the little ones may release their inhibitions and hence behave better at home. But educators cannot permit the students to dic-

tate the course of study unless they are prepared to confess that they are nothing but chaperons, supervising an
aimless, trial-and-error process which is chiefly valuable
because it keeps young people from doing something
worse. The free elective system as Mr. Eliot introduced
it at Harvard and as Progressive Education adapted it to
lower age levels amounted to a denial that there was content to education. Since there was no content to education, we might as well let students follow their own bent.
They would at least be interested and pleased and would
be as well educated as if they had pursued a prescribed
course of study. This overlooks the fact that the aim of
education is to connect man with man, to connect the
present with the past, and to advance the thinking of the
race. If this is the aim of education, it cannot be left to
the sporadic, spontaneous interests of children or even of
undergraduates.[5]

Social Effects of the "New Education"

Most civilized men have appreciated the fact that they
must decide certain things for their children, at least until
the children attain sufficient capacity to decide for themselves. True freedom is the freedom of self-discipline, a freedom to choose within acceptable standards and values. Take
away the values and standards, take away the discipline, and
meaningful freedom is taken away as well.

In the education of our future leaders, we might well remember that men without moral discipline, men who deny

---

[5] Robert M. Hutchins, *The Higher Learning in America,* pp. 70-71.

any allegiance to standards higher than themselves, are likely to become leaders or to follow leaders who stand for nothing but brute force. As modern educationists struggle to "free" man from the old "limiting" standards, they justify their stance with constant reference to the democratic way of life. Any attempt to impose standards is thus labeled "undemocratic." It is worth remembering that democracy is a *political* concept and that all applications of that concept to other aspects of human life, education included, are the tacit admission that the architects of the new order intend that all values will ultimately be political values. In all of the endless talk about "growth" that fills our discussion of education, we steadfastly refuse to answer the one central question, growth for what purpose?

"Growth for what purpose?" We are told at various times that the goals include "self-expression," "life adjustment," "adaptation to daily living." The school seems to have become a center in which the individual is told that he will be subjected to no disciplinary standards, that he can be "himself."

How does the student realize himself? By adjusting to his peers and to the society around him. He must learn to "get along." He fulfills himself in his capacity to work with others . . . in and of himself he is nothing. If he has strivings or attitudes not in conformity with the world around him, he must "adjust." He, not society, is in the wrong. The individual, stripped of the standards of self-discipline which would allow him to be his unique self, is thus educated in the new value of conformity.

How can this conformity be described except as a mass of standardized mediocrity? How can such a society hope to generate the leadership necessary for its continued existence? The choice, finally, is between discipline and disaster.

6. The Perpetual Adolescent

BY WAY OF A DECLINE in standards, in intellect, and in discipline, we have bred a new sort of social animal, for whom the educationist's aim is not achievement but "adjustment." That word has come to mean a number of things. To some educators, "adjustment" originally meant the provision of a modern "functional" program of high school education for those who would not receive college or vocational training beyond high school. Roughly 60 per cent of American high school children were assumed to fall into that category. But, as one of those educators, Dr. Harl Douglass, has commented, "It is coming to be believed by more and more people that a good program for that 60 per cent might well be an excellent program for all American youth." Dr. Douglass appears to be suggesting that "adjustment" is now aimed at slowing those of college caliber to the mental pace of the majority.

Our American educational ideal is being molded more and more to that image. We now place special emphasis upon training the dropouts, upon making the curriculum so soft that no one can flunk. Thus, we are caught up in one of the fundamental "democratic" dilemmas of our age. It is no longer enough merely to provide schools for all; today we must determine what purpose those schools are to serve.

71

If we make our schools sufficiently mindless to accommodate those least able, we run the grave risk of turning out a totally mindless graduate. Such a solution should be unsatisfactory, unless we wish democracy to mean the rule of the uniformly ignorant and incompetent. Perhaps we've toiled unduly over defects and weaknesses and shortcomings, to the grave neglect of talents and virtues and achievements. If we wish our schools to be only shelters for idle youth, we must recognize the frankly revolutionary premise which underlies such a system. The logic of such "democratic" pedagogy implies a total structural change of traditional American society.

The American Adolescent

The American child is famous throughout the world for having never confronted authority in his entire life. He typically is raised by parents who are permissive beyond belief, is educated in a school system in which the teacher is known to have no power to compel order, and is entertained by a television set whose programming and advertising constantly cater to the most childish of fads. Perhaps the poor parents of such children should not be held fully accountable. Not only are they contending against the spirit of the age in any attempt to assert discipline, but in late years parents have been informed by the child psychologist that attempts to impose standards of discipline on their children will interfere with proper "development."

Not only are we bending every effort to make spoiled brats of our young people; we carefully prolong this anti-training period by keeping our children in school far longer than do most other societies. The nature of that schooling seems to aggravate further the whole situation, directly interfering with the transfer of ethical and cultural traditions from one generation to the next. The parents are told that the schools will do the job, and then the schools do nothing of the kind.

Often, the hardest working and most intelligent parents have the greatest difficulty in raising their children. Many of the most financially successful people in our industrial society are busied by virtue of their success. They have a great deal of money, but very little time to offer their children. All the advantages of work discipline, which the fathers learned so well, are denied the rising generation largely because of the affluence, success, and hurried pace of the fathers. A road without challenges or responsibilities becomes the road too easily traveled by many of America's young people. Here, again, the temptation is to delegate the responsibility to professional educators whose underlying philosophy makes its proper discharge impossible.

Once the family was bound together through working at common tasks, often including the tasks of feeding and clothing and housing the family. What comparable experience is available to the young person of today? In the absence of meaningful moral experience and hard work, today's young are directed toward material gratification of their passing interests. The promises of our technological civilization and the philosophy of our educational system both contribute to the malady.

To pin one's hope for happiness to the fact that "the world is so full of a number of things" is an appropriate sentiment for a "Child's Garden of Verse." For the adult to maintain an exclusive Bergsonian interest in "the perpetual gushing forth of novelties" would seem to betray an inability to mature. The effect on a mature observer of an age so entirely turned from the One to the Many as that in which we are living must be that of a prodigious peripheral richness joined to a great central void.[1]

That great central void to which Babbitt refers is painfully evident in the breakdown of family and the collapse of social standards. Still, we continue the "protection" of our young from any responsibility or reality. Teen-agers are not to be punished as adults, though they commit the same crimes. The open warfare between weary adults and abusive teen-agers continues on all fronts and has today been elevated into a pseudocultural movement. We bribe our children with far more money than we would ever have believed possible to spend, and then are amazed when their childish tastes, backed with these immense amounts of purchasing power, set standards of taste in entertainment at steadily lower and lower levels. We expect no responsibility in our children and all too often get what we expect.

"Adjustment"

In the name of "progressive education" we have emancipated the young from all traditional authority. We label the result "freedom," completely forgetting how difficult it is

---

[1] Irving Babbitt, *Rousseau and Romanticism,* p. 277.

to be *responsibly* free. We have encouraged a revolt against standards and against discipline by the young people, who ultimately will be asked to pay a high price for their incapacities.

One of the worst culprits in consigning these young people to their lifelong fate has been our system of formal education. Many educationists insist that the mediocre standards in today's school are "set by an intellectual aristocracy" and are far too high! They regard the minimal standards of literacy imposed by industry or by higher education as unwarranted demands. Reading, writing, and arithmetic have become suspect in the minds of many. Consider, for example, the sentiments of one junior high school principal:

Through the years we've built a sort of halo around reading, writing, and arithmetic. We've said they were for everybody. . . .

We've made some progress in getting rid of that slogan. But every now and then some mother with a Phi Beta Kappa award or some employer who has hired a girl who can't spell stirs up a fuss about the schools . . . and ground is lost. . . .

When we come to the realization that not every child has to read, figure, write, and spell . . . that many of them either cannot or will not master these chores . . . then we shall be on the road to improving the junior high curriculum.

Between this day and that a lot of selling must take place. But it's coming. We shall some day accept the thought that it is just as illogical to assume that every boy must be able to read as it is that each one must be able to perform on the violin, that it is no more reasonable to require that each girl shall spell well than it is that each shall bake a good cherry pie. . . .[2]

There in capsule form is standardless education carried to its logical conclusion!

Such an attitude, at first glance, is hard to understand, that is, if one assumes that the purpose of education is to educate. But if one believes that the purpose of education is to achieve only "adjustment," then much of the educationist mumbo-jumbo begins to fall into place. Mortimer Smith also quotes a letter from a state department of education informing parents who plan to teach their children at home that under no circumstances will they be allowed to do so:

> No matter how competent the parents may be, the child who obtains his schooling at home is not having an experience equivalent to that of the child who goes to an authorized school. The school program does not consist only of mastering the 3 R's and the various content subjects. Perhaps the most important part of the school program is the association in a group. . . . Practically all American living today is a cooperative affair. Children have to learn to take turns and to share. Group discipline and group loyalties have to be developed.[3]

"Adjustment" rather than learning would appear to be the wave of the future!

---

[2] As quoted by Mortimer Smith, *The Diminished Mind*, pp. 36-37.
[3] *Ibid.*, pp. 49-50.

All self-discipline leading to independence is denied the young person in such a system. The institutions of higher learning in this country constantly complain of the quality of material they are given to "educate." It seems that the knowledge of geography, history, grammar, spelling, arithmetic, science, or what-have-you, as achieved by the products of our public school system, is so slight as to be a constant embarrassment to them and to the institutions of higher learning and business firms where the well entertained but poorly educated young people eventually go. I use the phrase "well entertained" with good reason.

On reading about the uninhibited conduct of certain grade-school classes, with free discussion, finger painting, group games, or whatever the youngsters want to do, an older man said: "That's not a new feature of education. They had that when I was a boy. They called it 'recess.' "[4]

The "Old-Fashioned" Way

Meanwhile, some educationists insist that obeying the teacher or striving to master a difficult subject is negative in its impact upon the child. What an older society viewed as sound mental, moral, or intellectual training is today dismissed as "old-fashioned." Indeed, some of the "progressive" educators have carried their noneducation to lengths that are increasingly repudiated by more and more people concerned with education. Today the term "progressive"

---

[4] Calvin D. Linton, "Higher Education: The Solution—Or Part of the Problem?" *Christianity Today*, Feb. 16, 1968.

often is held in bad repute. Yet, many educational policies
stemming from the same philosophic roots continue to
dominate much of our educational structure.

The same problem continues to face us. How do we lead
a child toward maturity except by initiating him into the
demands and standards of adult life? The old-fashioned
answer to that question rested upon definite standards, enforced through definite discipline.

During my boyhood in the mountains of Colorado, I was
privileged to attend a one-room, one-teacher school that met
the needs of children in all eight elementary grades. Admittedly, I was fortunate to have a remarkable teacher of
great character and strong personality, who was then and
remains a profound influence on my life. Yet, without the
benefits of swimming pools, of guidance counselors, of the
1,001 other such items now assumed to be "essential" to
education, we children of that school (incidentally, a cross
section of well-to-do and very poor) managed to learn our
reading and writing and arithmetic, while learning to respect adults, respect one another, and finally to respect
ourselves. Throughout, the standards we were expected to
maintain were never in doubt. We also knew at all times
who was running the school!

Such schools and such teachers have been the tradition
rather than the exception in this country. In fact, much of
what we now call "juvenile delinquency" would have been
subject to quick solution in the woodshed of an earlier day.
But then, such a system as I am describing was based upon
standards and discipline, viewing children as individuals,

individuals important for their own sake, individuals destined to assume a responsible place in the community. Today, we extend no such courtesy to our young people.

Necessity for Individual Discipline and Standards

The development of the individual presupposes the development of a strong capacity to judge the world around him and a genuine self-commitment moving the individual to act on the basis of that judgment. As Nietzsche described the process, what is required is self-mastery, the individual's imposition on himself of a style, a restraint, a proper form of behavior.

When the educationists announce their intention to teach the young "adjustment to life," the first question which arises is how "life" might be defined. If by "life" the educationist means only adjustment to a pattern of political conformity in which man no longer has problems because he no longer has aspirations, then such a definition must be dismissed. A truly individual adjustment to life must reflect not mere conformity, but good and bad, tragedy and comedy. Without room for man to be a hero, to pursue an ideal, to become uniquely himself, there is no opportunity for the individual to be truly human. When men drift rather than strive, the direction of that drift is always toward barbarism, toward a decline of that sense of style and self-discipline which makes for the civilized man.

Thus, a great civilization is no more enduring than are the proper conventions among its citizens. The child in whom good habits are not inculcated becomes the child in whom bad habits have filled the void. Often, the basis for right conduct is less a reasoned position than it is a matter of habit. Habit in this sense is a reflection of the wide experience of the race, passed on by disciplined and demanding standards to each generation as they grow toward maturity.

The acquisition of such habits is never easy, since it demands much from both pupil and teacher. In fact, many men never seem to learn the lesson. "Experience keeps a hard school, but fools will learn in no other." Yet most of us have a hard time learning from self-experience, let alone the experience of others. The business of being human is never easy, and our young deserve all the help they can get as they strive for maturity and the formation of civilized habits. What that striving has taught the Western world is that the really valuable power in this universe is not the power over other men, but the power over oneself. This power reflects not only knowledge, but restraint; not only energy, but will. To maintain standards means to develop the capacity to choose and reject, to have so disciplined one's attitudes as to have established an ethical center uniquely oriented to self, producing right conduct in the individual no matter what the conduct of the world around him might be.

If the child is to grow toward such self-discipline, the formation of proper habits must, as Aristotle says, precede reason. No child is truly free to choose until he has become sufficiently disciplined to see the full implications of his choice. When we limit the formation of proper habit, we blunt the power of discrimination in the young, thus binding rather than freeing. It becomes clear that genuine learning and civilization of our young is a process which takes place only when the proper exercise of authority, the authority of standards and discipline, is present in education.

The necessity for such discipline is especially apparent when we consider the unique attribute which human beings call *mind*. The word "mind" implies far more than the human brain. All patterns of thought, all moral and aesthetic judgments, are the work of this amazingly individual quality possessed by each of us. All value judgments, all civilized behavior, stem from the individual's mind within which symbols are understood, evaluated, and applied in one's behavior. The idea of education is to enlarge that process, not merely by the passive reception of ideas, but by the mind's development of the capacity to sort out, choose between, and evaluate those symbols and ideas. In short, all meaningful knowledge is knowledge which we have "made our own"; until the individual acquires the necessary discipline of mind to do so, he has not been truly educated.

Some authority must be present in education in which the superior capacity of the teacher demonstrates subtle distinctions to the relatively untrained and undisciplined mentality of the student. In this sense, values are constantly *recreated* in the mind of each individual. That process of re-creation is education, and demands that the teacher be sufficiently disciplined to have mastered the concepts and the processes, also demanding that the student be sufficiently disciplined to achieve the same ultimate self-mastery.

In the old academic term for various subjects, "disciplines," the idea is implicit that the mind must be sufficiently developed and trained to *think* before it can recognize what is of value and what is valueless. True development of the individual rests on that capacity to distinguish and choose within his mind and heart. It is that capacity to choose which makes us human. It is the removal of that disciplined capacity to choose, as fostered by modern education, which would make of us mere "adjusted" automatons.

Such choice is never easy. Life itself is never easy, demanding obedience, renunciation, and the expenditure of great effort if it is to be truly meaningful. Throughout the ages philosophers have demonstrated the necessity for sacrifice, for self-mastery. Yet, we are now told that man need not master himself to be "happy." Apparently more material goods and politically controlled "security" are to make self-discipline no longer necessary. True happiness lies upon a different path. We must learn to put ourselves into our work, to master ourselves, if we will be truly civilized.

It must not be the business of the teacher to teach the young only what the young wish to learn. Instead the experience of the human race must be offered to the young while proper habits are developed, allowing these young individuals to assume their own self-disciplined place in civilized society. In this connection, we are all the teachers of the young. The churches as well as the schools have an obligation in this regard, and the primary obligation must rest with the parent and the home. The idea must be conveyed that good hard work is preferable to "getting by," that people receive from life exactly what they put in, that privileges and obligations go hand in hand.

As the schools pursue this general disciplinary function, they also must pursue the disciplines of form, number, and language. Reading, writing, and arithmetic are far from out-dated, no matter what the opinions of the professional educationists. When these disciplines are set aside in favor of "personality development" or "group adjustment," the school is no longer serving its function. The school must be far more than an elaborately contrived and terribly expensive baby-sitting facility. It must first and foremost be an institution designed to impart sound moral and intellectual discipline to the citizens of tomorrow. Such discipline must be a discipline of both mind and heart, reflecting an external discipline leading to more important, internal, *self-imposed* discipline. Such a system would produce true individuals, complete human beings.

7. Why Institutionalize Our Errors?

WHATEVER SHORTCOMINGS may be said to exist in American elementary and secondary education are largely traceable to the philosophic errors discussed earlier in these pages.

For example, the unfortunate emphasis upon *how* to teach, rather than *what* to teach, stems directly from two pernicious ideas: 1. There can be no fixed truth, no ultimate standard, thus making impossible all "knowledge" in the traditional sense. 2. The search for the latest version of truth (i.e., the *method* of that search) is thought to be not merely a means, but the new end itself.

Our prospective elementary and secondary teachers are often given large quantities of professional "Education" courses and courses offering only a smattering of different disciplines, leaving little time for genuine education in any discipline. The result? Much of a prospective teacher's first twelve years in school reflects the lack of intellectual standards and discipline described earlier. When he goes to college to prepare himself to be a teacher, he finds that "teacher certification" requirements largely interfere with his receiving a genuine education. Should our teacher go on to graduate school, he again often finds himself surrounded by professors of education. Thus the prospective teacher finds himself submerged in the educational bureaucracy and cut off from much of what constitutes education in any discipline. In this way the educationist mentality becomes the force which often actually controls public education. This force generally demonstrates itself to be almost totally unfamiliar with standards of genuine education, totally preoccupied with the development and maintenance of largely meaningless technical requirements and course work.

Similar pressures generated by our wrong-headed modern philosophy have undercut discipline and standards in many of our schools. Worse yet, these errors have become institutionalized through the centralization and bigness pressing so heavily upon student and teacher alike throughout much of our educational structure.

The Enlargement of Educational Responsibility

The parent can and should look beyond himself for specialized help in a proper education of his child, but neither parent nor teacher should be confused about the parent's ultimate responsibility or the proper role of the school in the upbringing of the young. Unfortunately, such distinctions have blurred in our society. The growth of the public school system has been more than matched by a bureaucracy to regulate its workings. As the system has grown, elected officials have felt compelled to place its administration in "expert" hands, a control generally centered in state departments of education. Public school teachers through the high school level are now expected to take certain "Education" courses serving as indoctrination in the "new" philosophy and methodology of the dominant bureaucracy. Our population expansion further enlarges the role of the educationists in our society until they dominate our gigantic and expensive educational structure and assume the functions of family and church as well. We find ourselves well advanced toward a new educational structure, and a new social structure.

The Push Toward Centralization

It is quite natural that there should be some blurring of function between the home and the school, since both should properly require discipline and both play an important role in any educational process. But tremendous new problems develop when both functions are undertaken by the school. For the educationist bureaucracy, education is no longer a result to be achieved, but instead has become a subject to be institutionalized. Is it desirable for the school to so expand its responsibility? Even if it were desirable, can the school hope to discharge such responsibility?

The answer to both questions appears to be "no." The reason we have been able to muddle along with no more disastrous results than we have suffered from this usurpation of authority rests with the magnificent teachers in our schools whose personality and skill allow them to function in an atmosphere increasingly alien to true education. These fortunately numerous teachers have been willing to fight the battle despite the bureaucracy in which they are entombed, and the public apathy which so commonly greets them.

Another result of the growing educationist bureaucracy has been that our schools have become progressively less oriented to the education of individuals and more oriented to the education of the "masses." We now seem to turn out a "socialized" product, certified as socially acceptable by the appropriate diploma. The bureaucracy has succumbed to its own propaganda to the point of encouraging centralization and consolidation according to a master plan. Since the Second World War, a process of consolidation has taken place; small, locally-oriented school districts have been absorbed into larger and larger school systems, the better to facilitate "planning." What has actually taken place is a process whereby schools have been removed further from community and parental control, while larger "plants," larger staffs, and larger educationist blueprints have been imposed on the long-suffering taxpayer and the much-abused students. In the process, the small schools being closed were often superior to the new and larger schools taking their place.

When centralization is carried to its logical conclusion, when the educationist bureaucracy has had the fullest possible play for its ideas, what results have we experienced? New York City, a city which has given its educational bureaucracy vast authority and vast amounts of money, today offers an educational product which is frequently so inferior that people seek out private schools for their children or flee from the negative city environment altogether. Things have reached the point in which school often is not even convened, while various groups contend for bureaucratic control. The central question now seems to have become not "How can we best educate our children?" but "Who shall rule?"

Judging from some reports coming from around the United States, the time may come when we will suffer professors' strikes in our institutions of higher learning just as today we are suffering teachers' strikes in more and more of our public elementary and secondary schools. It seems that once we allow bigness to progress beyond a certain point, the reactions stemming from such monolithic power will crop up throughout society.

Even when we manage to keep school in session, the problem of bigness haunts us. In James B. Conant's widely accepted study of the American high school, he described high schools with graduating classes of less than 100 students as "too small to allow a diversified curriculum except at exorbitant expense." Thus, these small schools were, in Conant's opinion, "one of the serious obstacles to good secondary education throughout most of the United States." Mr. Conant's solution? More bigness, more centralization.

It is true that a larger school provides more specialized teaching and more staff specialists. Each student finds himself more counseled and tested. But it is also true that in the process the individual teacher steadily loses his personal contact with the students as more and more of his functions are taken over by outside "specialists." Students and teachers alike are involved in more and more activities outside the classroom while less of what has been traditionally called "teaching," the close pupil-teacher relationship, seems possible in our super-sized educational structure.

As teacher and student alike have suffered in the new educational environment, the bureaucracy has prospered. Federal aid to education has further accelerated the whole process, helping to produce an increasingly dangerous situation:

It is not too much to say that in the past fifty years public education in the United States has been in the hands of revolutionaries. To grasp the nature of their attempted revolution, we need only realize that in the past every educational system has reflected to a great extent the social and political constitution of the society which supported it. This was assumed to be a natural and proper thing, since the young were to be trained to take places in the world that existed around them. They were "indoctrinated" with this world because its laws and relations were those by which they were expected to order their lives. In the period just mentioned, however, we have witnessed something never before seen in the form of a systematic attempt to undermine a society's traditions and beliefs through the educational establishment which is usually employed to maintain them. There has been an extraordinary occurrence, a virtual educational coup d'etat carried out by a specially inclined minority. This minority has been in essence a cabal, with objectives radically different from those of the state which employed them. An amazing feature of the situation has been how little they have cared to conceal these objectives. On more than one occasion they have issued a virtual call to arms to use publicly created facilities for the purpose of actualizing a concept of society not espoused by the people. The result has been an educational system not only intrinsically bad but increasingly at war with the aims of the community which authorizes it. . . .[1]

The School as an Agency of Social Reform

The revolutionary impact of the educationist philosophy described by Richard Weaver centers on the attempt to junk the traditional standards and substitute totally new goals in their place. The process of that philosophic departure from standards has already been described at some length. Innumerable examples surround us on virtually every hand. The principal effect of this departure from standards has been an assault upon individual personality.

In place of teaching the young to form their own opinions, today we offer social indoctrination, enthusing endlessly about "enrichment" and "freedom" and yet in many cases offering our young people only the dullest possible conformity. The present philosophic assumptions common within higher education often deny the idea of inner personality. Listen to the new method stated most frankly by John Dewey himself, writing in *Democracy and Education:*

> The idea of perfecting an "inner" personality is a sure sign of social divisions. What is called inner is simply that which does not connect with others—which is not capable of free and full communication. What is termed spiritual culture has usually been futile, with something rotten about it, just because it has been conceived as a

---

[1] Richard M. Weaver, *Visions of Order*, pp. 260-261.

thing which a man might have internally—and therefore exclusively. What one is as a person is what one is as associated with others, in a free give and take of intercourse.

What's wrong with society? The old and negative ideas stressing individual personality! Give us enough money and let us adjust the child. Then all will be well. To what must the child adjust? To "social democracy," to finding his values within society. In fact, the replacement of all norms and the replacement of all individual personality is to be achieved within the system because the new means of arriving at norms and standards, at truth, is through the new methodology. Society will vote, society will establish a "consensus," and from that consensus will come the new standards, the new definitions of truth, the new social man as replacement for the individual. Such a system violates both of the canons necessary for genuine education. It violates the individual's freedom to choose and the framework of standards and values within which meaningful individual choice may take place.

A society pursuing such educational goals is likely to become a society oriented toward action rather than thought. Such a society places a premium upon masses of humanity, upon sheer body weight rather than intellectual weight. In place of moral and intellectual standards, numbers and crowd psychology are to determine our future course. We are beginning to live through the first painful results of such a disastrous philosophy, as evidenced by the violence and mob psychology which today is commonplace both in-

side and outside our academic community. Thus, violence
has become our means for making decisions and solving
"problems."

Emerson once remarked, "Men ride on a thought, as if
each bestrode an invisible horse, which, if it became visible,
all their seemingly mad plunging motions would be explained." Surely this observation could be applied to our
present society. In our traditional system of higher learning, education was conceived as passing along the cardinal
principles and values of civilization, but our modern assumption today is that we have no values worth passing on.
If this is the idea we give our young people to ride on, can
we be surprised when they act as if there were no values?
If the intellectual community will no longer regard itself
as primarily devoted to the pursuit of truth, can we be
surprised when our young are no longer willing to listen
to the members of the academic community?

When we take freedom to mean nothing more than the
absence of external control, we are paving the way for the
most dangerous anarchy imaginable. Meaningful freedom
involves the presence of internal restraint and sound judgment. Without these restraints and that capacity for judgment, we open the door to mass action in virtually every
area of our society. This is not the achievement of freedom,
it is a return to barbarism.

The extended criticisms laid at the door of American
education prompt this question: "If things are so bad, why
is the system still yielding so many first-rate students, so
many fine young men and women?" The answer is easy:

The saving grace of our educational structure is the stubborn virtue and determined excellence of many teachers who continue to function well under admittedly adverse circumstances. Students are quick to identify a good teacher when they meet one. A real teacher never stops, but continues in school and out, by precept and example, to set high standards of discipline and character. The old teacher-pupil relationship of one-to-one, the teacher and the taught, implying standards and discipline and the meeting of two distinctly individual personalities, remains the only real answer to the problem.

The Numbers Problem in Higher Education

The philosophic shortcomings of American mass education form a core of problems for higher education as well. Often the most severe criticism of American secondary education comes from the liberal arts faculties of our colleges and universities. They decry the intellectual material being sent them by the secondary schools and are openly contemptuous of the Education departments on their own campuses. Yet many of these critics of educationism are themselves empire builders of a sort. They are often the first to suggest that more and more young people should go to college whether qualified or not. This is to be achieved by sufficiently lowering standards so that no one need be rejected and no one need fail to measure up. The result in practice tends to be a steadily lowering rate of standards, a steady decline in the educational system's capacity to treat its students as individuals. When such college teachers criticize

the anti-intellectualism of the "educationist" and complain
of the spotty quality of all too many students, they may
actually be criticizing the final result of the same relativist,
materialist, collectivist philosophy which higher education
itself often espouses.

Whatever the causes, some college classrooms seem filled
with students who cannot handle solid college material,
students who feel they have a "right" to be in college
whether or not they are qualified or motivated. The problem is made more pressing because the total number of students, qualified or unqualified, grows steadily greater. In
1956 there were less than 3 million students in college; ten
years later the number had doubled. Some estimates suggest that the next ten years will see the number doubled
again.

America has long been committed to the idea of universal education. The question today: Is having everyone
in school synonymous with giving everyone an education?
In actual fact, a part of our increased college enrollment
has less to do with education than with the painful fact
that no socially acceptable alternative to college attendance
exists for an intelligent secondary school graduate. Consider
the social standing of the alternatives for an 18-year-old
high school grad—the army? a job?

Today America has apparently undertaken a commitment
to send everyone to college, just as 40 years ago it promised
a universal high school education and 40 years before that
aspired to offer an eighth grade diploma to all youngsters.
New colleges and universities are coming into existence at

the rate of one a week. This may well be regarded as a worthwhile ambition in an era of "rising expectations," *if the quality of the education thus offered has real value.* But if we make a college education available to all only by lowering standards and making that education meaningless, we are only deceiving ourselves.

Such "mass" oriented institutions run the risk of becoming merely custodial rather than educational. In such an environment, teaching an individual to think for himself may easily be lost in the shuffle of massive enrollments, watered-down survey courses, and the rest of the techniques which deny primacy to the individual.

If America should demand that everyone attend college and true standards be damned, and if America builds more and larger institutions of higher learning of a sort to accommodate such a process, we shall be taking the next disastrous step in the further institutionalization of our philosophic errors. Surely we do not need more institutional giantism for its own sake. We have great need to bring our existing educational structure back within the scope of the individual student.

8. The Multiversity

THE PROPER GOAL of education is the development of the individual; and the great task is to bring the educational structure back to that purpose. Unfortunately, the trend continues in the opposite direction. The multiversity, to use the term coined by Clark Kerr, would appear to be a modern hybrid with a scale of values oriented toward everything but the individual student.

Formerly, the university was regarded as a sanctuary for original and independent thinking. Many centers of higher learning today seem willing to prostitute themselves in pursuit of public funds. Indeed, the race for funds goes far beyond that; it also includes the development of a curriculum featuring the vocational training demanded by the professions and the business community. In short, many of our institutions of higher learning are directing themselves not toward independent inquiry and the development of inquiring individuals, but instead are providing the institutions of our society, both public and private, with the properly "prepared" (though not necessarily educated) graduates needed to staff our social structure. An "assembly line" is thus set in motion, as the demands of both public and private institutional giants shape the higher learning in America.

Traditionally, academicians have abandoned the market place to better pursue their work; but it has been suggested that "modern America has thrust its academicians back into the commercial arena." Clark Kerr, in *The Uses of the University,* has defined the modern university as "a mechanism . . . held together by administrative rules and powered by money." He adds that "it only pays to produce knowledge if through production it can be put into use better and faster." If everything within the academic community is for sale to the highest bidder, if concentrations of power, public and private, are allowed to establish all the criteria for what constitutes education, then we should not be surprised when bigness displaces the individual and "workability" replaces values.

Meanwhile, the multiversity grows by leaps and bounds. Administration is becoming one of the great academic problems of our times, as "specialists" are added to handle fund raising, public relations, purchasing, and the myriad other technical problems which we have insisted upon making a part of higher education. Under the banner of "public service," the giantism of the modern multiversity is becoming the commonplace of American education.

Impersonality

The severe impact of the multiversity upon the student is described by two Berkeley professors who have faced the situation firsthand:

The architects of the multiversity simply have not
solved the problem of how to build an institution which
not only produces knowledge and knowledgeable people
with useful skills but which also enriches and enlightens
the lives of its students. . . . By any reasonable standard,
the multiversity has not taken its students seriously . . .
to many students the whole system seems a perversion
of an educational community into a factory designed for
the mass processing of men into machines.[1]

Often, the impact of the multiversity is equally severe
upon the professors. As massive enrollments and expendi-
tures have necessitated a great and growing educational
bureaucracy, the traditional small "community of scholars"
has gradually deteriorated in many institutions into a large
group of salaried employees. The great and growing numbers which the multiversity attempts to serve impose great
burdens upon student, professor, and administrator alike.
And as they rush through their appointed rounds in an
effort to keep the gigantic system in operation, they find
that each new fall brings larger and larger crowds of students to be digested by the system. The tremendous numbers involved have forced many institutions to use IBM
cards and other means of mass processing, further widening
the gap between the institution and the individual. The
impersonality beginning with registration is maintained in
giant survey classes and concluded with anonymous gradua-

[1] Sheldon S. Wolin and John H. Schaar, "The Abuses of the Multiversity," Seymour Martin Lipset and Sheldon S. Wolin, eds., *The Berkeley
Student Revolt* (New York: Doubleday Anchor, 1965).

tions. In many cases students and professors never come to know one another—indeed, the products of such a system are not always worth knowing.

When any institutional framework deals with thousands of persons each day, it is not surprising if there is neither time nor resources for an individualized approach. Yet, can the development of independent judgment and a genuine insight into the human condition be accomplished without a close interaction of teacher and pupil? The answer is "no." Thus, many students who are attending the multiversity in search of an education are being deceived. They find themselves neglected in an institution primarily directed toward the procurement of Federal and foundation research grants and the development of the proper institutional "image."

College and university alike seem to suffer from the same disease. As Robert Hutchins put the case:

> The reason is that the students, who have been lured to the college by its proclaimed dedication to liberal education, find on their arrival that the reality is quite different. In reality, the college is, except in size, the same as a university, devoted to training and not to education. . . . Unless the American university is completely reorganized and reoriented it can only mishandle and frustrate the students who reject the mindless mechanism of the academic assembly line; the students, in short, are looking for an education.[2]

A part of the problem, of course, is due to the sheer magnitude of our institutions of higher learning. Such giant-

---

[2] Robert M. Hutchins, Los Angeles *Times,* Oct. 31, 1966.

ism makes adaptation to change and to individual needs especially difficult. But merely escaping from the giant university to the smaller college is no guarantee of success. The colleges are becoming in many cases little more than satellites to the great universities. Their ideas and attitudes often originate in the large universities; their teachers are usually trained there.

Some institutions are attempting a so-called "cluster-college" approach for re-establishment of faculty-student contact. But the expense involved leads administrators back toward the "greater efficiency" of centralization. They argue that the savings in planning physical facilities for large blocks of students can then be applied in procurement of more and better personnel. In their view, large size becomes a solution to educational problems rather than a problem in itself.

It is true that effective higher education requires fine intellect and scholarship in its teachers, and such teachers are difficult to attract to the small campus when all the money and most of the prestige lie in the great multiversities. In either case, it remains extremely difficult for students to contact fine teachers. Many of the small schools cannot attract such men, and many of the large schools who can attract them are so beset with vast numbers that teacher and pupil seldom have personal contact.

Size introduces a further complication. Many people recognize that a proper background in the so-called "liberal arts" is essential to the development of the whole man, whatever his profession might be. Attempts have been made to mass produce such education through the use of the universal survey course. The result often is a student who knows something about everything and nothing about anything.

Each professor and each department want the whole time of the student so that he can be thoroughly trained in the professor's or the department's specialty. Since it is obviously impossible for the student's whole time to be spent in this way, the course of study is determined by a process of pulling and hauling and finally emerges as a sort of checkerboard across which the bewildered student moves, absorbing from each square, it is hoped, a little of something that each professor or department has to offer him.[3]

Specialization

Not all of our problems should be laid at the door of mere size and numbers. Higher education labors under other handicaps as well. The pressures of the system drive the good teacher toward such increasingly narrow specialization that the information ceases to be readily communicable to students. Our highly technical modern world demands specialization. But vocational specialization without understanding of the humanities and liberal arts affords a limited perspective on life. Narrow specialization tends to dehumanize. A man's work is a vital part of his life; but unless that work is kept in touch with the realities of the human condition and in contact with a higher purpose,

---

[3] Robert M. Hutchins, *The Conflict in Education*, pp. 60-61.

all difference between man and automaton will have been removed.

Specialized knowledge in the Western world has accomplished miracles through increasing human control over physical environment. Man has achieved power in the process, a power being concentrated in the governmental and private institutional giants of our time. Rewards are high for the specialist. In such a process, however, we run a grave risk of losing the capacities which make us human. A young student of great ability easily may pass through his entire education without encountering the reality of the human condition or establishing his self-identity. Instead, he moves from one superficial consideration to the next, always dependent upon "expert" and "fashionable" opinion, "objectively" studying nothing but the "facts."

Superspecialization further requires a seemingly infinite variety of course offerings in the curriculum. It *is* true that men are different, but surely there are features of the human condition which are universal and which override all specialization.

Only by maintaining a balance between our experimental bent and our loyalty to the ageless wisdom of our tradition can we hope to remain culturally in the Western orbit. The distinguishing mark of the educated man is his sense of continuity and the awareness of his heritage. As Professor Josef Pieper has the courage to affirm in an age of specialization, a man must be able to comprehend the *totality of existence*.[4]

---

[4] Thomas Molnar, *The Future of Education,* p. 157.

Specialization also serves as a shield for many within the educational community who do not appear primarily concerned with education. There are some who pursue erudition for its own sake, divorced from any meaning in human existence. They conceal their lack of a philosophy of life behind an endless search for facts. Educational bureaucrats often seem to reflect the victory of the modern specialist over the universally educated man.

But this creates an extraordinarily strange type of man. . . . With a certain apparent justice he will look upon himself as "a man who knows." And in fact there is in him a portion of something which, added to many other portions not existing in him, does really constitute knowledge. This is the true inner nature of the specialist, who in the first years of this century has reached the wildest stage of exaggeration. The specialist "knows" very well his own tiny corner of the universe; he is radically ignorant of all the rest. . . . Previously, men could be divided simply into the learned and the ignorant. . . . But your specialist cannot be brought in under either of these two categories. He is not learned, for he is formally ignorant of all that does not enter into his specialty; but neither is he ignorant, because he is "a scientist," and "knows" very well his own tiny portion of the universe. We shall have to say that he is a learned ignoramus, which is a very serious matter, as it implies that he is a person who is ignorant, not in the fashion of the ignorant man, but with all the petulance of one who is learned in his own special lines.[5]

---

[5] José Ortega y Gasset, *The Revolt of the Masses,* pp. 111-112.

At least a portion of the excessive specialization of our time must be blamed upon the fetish of the doctoral degree. But a research degree is far from an assurance that a man is a qualified teacher. In fact, as Irving Babbitt warned forty years ago, "the work that leads to a doctor's degree is a constant temptation to sacrifice one's growth as a man to one's growth as a specialist."

The superspecialization demanded in our times often leaves the individual, as Ortega says, so specialized that he is ignorant in many facets of human existence, so ignorant that, outside his speciality, he reacts as an unqualified mass-man. Is it possible that professors who speak with such authority in areas outside their disciplines sometimes reflect that lack of training—proving themselves unqualified to exercise leadership outside their narrow specialization?

Publish or Perish

The drive toward superspecialization and the accompanying multiversity quest for "image," serving as means for reaping the appropriate financial rewards available through conformity to the pressures of the gigantic public and private institutional structure, have one of their most unfortunate manifestations in "publish or perish," the proliferation of research and publication for its own sake. One Stanford psychologist has suggested that

. . . before the turn of the century, it will be recognized that radical action is necessary to limit the outpouring of specialized and often trivial publications that even now all but inundate the offices of every academician.

. . . The most prestigeful colleges will begin by making rules forbidding their professors to publish until they have been on the faculty five or even 10 years. They will thus create a campus culture in which publishing is considered not good form.[6]

Though the professor may have had his tongue in cheek, there can be little doubt that a mass of trivial research tends to contaminate the academic atmosphere and bring legitimate research into disrepute. It also interferes with teaching. So long as the high road to academic success is thought to lie exclusively in research, we can scarcely expect faculty members to be properly concerned with the teaching function.

Writing, to be worthwhile, should flow naturally out of scholarship, not be imposed upon it, otherwise this forced labor acquires the status of Christmas cards and is counted, not read. If university administrators were required in their purgatory to read all of the trivia which their policies have produced, they would soon crowd the Gates of Hell clamoring for surcease.[7]

It is to the everlasting credit of a number of American colleges that they have not bowed to the pressures for research, but instead have kept teaching as their primary goal. Many of our multiversity complexes could profitably note the comparative lack of student unrest in the American col-

---

[6] "Stop Publishing or We'll All Perish," *The Stanford Observer*, March, 1968.

[7] A. H. Hobbs, "Sociology and Scholarship," *The University Scholar* (University of Pennsylvania), January, 1960.

lege as compared to the American university. An important reason for that difference could be an attitude in many colleges that teaching is a legitimate function of higher education. Independent scholarly inquiry and research are vital to our society and form an important part of our educational process, but we throw out the baby with the bath when we so overemphasize that function that we come to neglect the means for transmitting our increased knowledge to the rising generation.

Tenure and Promotion

The internal political situation surrounding tenure and promotion can also interfere with the educational process. The trustees of many educational institutions have yielded to faculty pressures until control of the institution is the prize to be won in an open contest between the professors and the administrators. Many administrative positions on campuses have fallen captive to faculty politics. Junior professors often depend for promotions upon senior departmental members whose self-interest leaves them poorly qualified to judge the merits of another professor.

Such forays into campus and departmental politics at the expense of teaching duties often are encouraged by the tenure situation. The tradition of tenure as a guarantee that the professor can conduct his research and publish his findings without censorship or fear for his job is a vital part of our academic heritage. But tenure was never intended as a protection for the lazy professor who read his last book while a graduate student; nor was its purpose to allow pro-

fessors to engage in politics while neglecting teaching responsibilities.

Collective Judgment and the Committee

Inside and outside the American academic community,
the committee mentality assaults us on every hand. The
highest rewards seem to go to organizers and co-ordinators
rather than to genuinely creative and original minds. Our
worship of institutions not only gives us the multiversity, but
also subjects us to nonthought by committee in the everyday conduct of our affairs.

> One glance at pedagogical literature reveals the col-
> lectivistic preoccupation: "Committee," "cooperation," "in-
> tegration," "teamwork," "group-project," "majority-objec-
> tives," "peer-group," "group-process," "group-imposed
> regulations," "group-determined penalty," "group-accept-
> ance," etc., etc., abound in articles, speeches, meetings,
> and school catalogues. Together with other ideological
> directives, they constitute the affirmation that God and in-
> dividual man do not exist apart from the collectivity.
> Moreover, they imply that man's adjustment to the col-
> lectivity is the supreme guarantee that he is not in error.[8]

Needless to say, committees are no better as teachers than as
administrators.

University teachers can be and frequently have been
vigorous educational forces. The really effective professors
prove to be those with a full understanding that genuinely
effective college teaching involves far more than lecturing

---

[8] Thomas Molnar, *The Future of Education,* p. 134.

before large survey classes and then quickly disappearing to the library or the faculty club. At least one aspect of the student uprising on campuses has been the teaching failure of the multiversity. In fact, the kind of student protest that emphasizes body English and mass movements in place of responsible individual thought and action demonstrates how little genuine education those students have received.

Students are more than great masses of IBM cards and administrative problems; they are far more than mere containers into which academic information should be dumped. Their value to society, their value to themselves, and their capacity for education are deeply affected by the capacity of the university to deal with them as individuals. If the many well-qualified and highly motivated administrators and professors within higher education are to be given an opportunity to reach their students, we must reverse the trend toward the multiversity with all its negative effects.

9. Academic Freedom for What?

PROFESSOR SIDNEY HOOK has quite justly criticized the great quantities of "sloppy rhetoric" poured forth on the subject of academic freedom. The overdiscussion of such a topic usually stems from chronic underdefinition, reflecting the painfully human trait of having the most to say on a subject when we are least sure what ought to be said.

Higher education is plagued by this lack of a workable definition for academic freedom, and this is rooted in a singular fact: *Never* has there been a formal statement of the relationship between the academic community and the rest of society. Is the academic community merely to teach our young? Or do we ask that it also discover new truths? Perhaps we also wish our teachers to serve as philosophers of the realm. In short, no lasting answer seems to have been given the questions: Should society decide what is taught in the grove académe? Should the academy decide society's course? Or, does some workable third alternative exist?

Perhaps the best means of getting at the relationship between the academy and society is to clarify what we have in mind when we discuss the education of the individual student. The student is the vital link between academy and society, since it is the student in whom both have a common stake. In the last analysis, we want one thing for the student: freedom—i.e., the achievement of that capacity for *internal* self-determination allowing him to become a whole man, his own man. How is this freedom to be achieved? It must be achieved through knowledge, through the development of a capacity for self-discipline, through an understanding of the obligations and privileges involved in life.

Freedom for the student surely cannot be attained without freedom for the teacher. Freedom to think, to challenge the common view on occasion, would therefore seem an absolute requirement if education is to achieve the full development of the individual student. Does this freedom to develop and state one's own views have no limitation? Many of those who discuss academic freedom insist that *any* restraint is unwarranted, since it interferes with a mysterious and ill-defined "universal dialogue." Others would insist that, while the freedom of *research* must be unlimited, society has a right to censor what its young people are taught. In effect, the teacher would be told, "Think what you like, but teach only what the majority approves."

Both of the above positions tend to be mere caricatures. Few actually advocate a literal freedom to teach *any* idea, however socially unacceptable it might be. An equally small number actually advocate a literal enforcement of censorship over the classroom teacher. The desirable norm lies somewhere between the two. Surely anyone qualified to teach the young should ideally already possess the inner freedom, the self-discipline, the necessary internal check of the truly civilized man, to maintain the standards of his ideas and values on such a high plane that parents should have no grounds for complaint. By the same token, parents should have sufficient confidence in the standards of teachers to allow them a free hand. If we as parents lack such confidence in the teachers, we should not allow them to teach our children at all.

The trouble lies in the fact that many teachers no longer seem to operate within the framework of values constituting civilized behavior. Such teachers seem to have adopted the totally relative standards so damaging to modern society. Parents are not to be blamed for recognizing that teachers who themselves lack standards of value are ill-prepared to impart the proper values to the young. This may explain why some parents desire to censor the classroom offerings of the teacher.

Such a desire may be understandable, but it is unacceptable if freedom for student and teacher is our goal. Merely substituting one set of wrong ideas for another set, trading license for repression, will not produce the desired effect.

Who Is the Teacher?

If the teacher is to lead the student on the high road to internal freedom, to his development as a unique person, he must be free himself; free to pursue his speculations, free to express the results of his findings. Such a teacher is more than an employee hired to teach the young. He becomes a seeker after truth, dedicated to explaining that truth to those who will follow. Academic freedom thus be-

comes an expression of sufficient confidence in the teacher to
allow that process to operate.

[Still, the search for truth carries with it the assumption
that truth *does* exist. The alleged "objective" approach of
many present-day educators contains no such assumption.
All ideas are to be presented to the student without that
evil of evils, the "value judgment." Such relativism finally
denies *all* values, thus destroying the framework of civilized
value within which meaningful individual choice must be
made.] Christ, Socrates, and the other great teachers of history had at least two things in common: they distinguished
between right and wrong; and they did not hesitate to announce that distinction to all who would listen. In short,
they recognized a framework of values.

There is also another historical lesson to be learned on the
necessity of values. Those societies denying the validity of a
value framework have invariably proven to be societies on
the decline. The Sophists who finally destroyed the Greeks
serve as a graphic example.

Unfortunately, truth will not necessarily rise to a dominant position in a totally "objective" teaching situation.
Teachers who fail to believe strongly enough in the existence of truth as a premise for their teaching often serve
as the ideal foils of those who would "stack the deck" against
the free choice of the individual. Witness the twentieth
century history of Russia or Germany, where totalitarian
control followed periods of so-called "free inquiry."

Ultimately, the teacher must be free to do his own thinking and the student must be free to choose what ideas he

will accept or reject. But the whole process of orderly thought becomes impossible unless some framework exists for the process of thinking. A completely relativistic stance is doomed to endless internal contradiction. If, as a relativist, a man insists that one opinion is as good as another, what defense has he against a totally contradictory view? If all views are equally valid, one man's denial is as sound as another's affirmation. Such thinking can only "agree to disagree" in an endless (and pointless) discussion foredoomed never to reach a conclusion. When academic freedom comes to mean only a freedom for endless disagreement—when the teacher and student no longer recognize a framework of values—thought itself ceases to exist and education in any real sense becomes impossible.

In a situation where "academic freedom" is so abused, it is small wonder that society finally balks at the prospect of the deforming educational process which results. Most men sense that freedom involves far more than the license to do as one pleases. Meaningful freedom has always implied responsibility, and responsibility demands self-control. Self-control presupposes guidelines within which the individual attempts to live in accord with accepted and acceptable standards. The denial of those standards and of the necessity for self-control in the name of "academic freedom" is as much a denial of true *freedom* for the individual as is an attempt to censor student and teacher in the classroom. Either way, genuine academic freedom suffers.

Much of the "sloppy rhetoric" on academic freedom to which Sidney Hook referred originates within the ranks of the "intellectual" community—authors, editors, critics, and scholars, many of whom tend to be enamored of their own company. This love affair is sufficiently ingrown that all too often these mutually congratulatory purveyors of "modern" thought have come to regard any criticism of their position as an assault upon "academic freedom." The strength of this delusion is verified by the spectacle of the many professors who seem to view themselves as part of an embattled non-conformist minority despite the fact that in many cases all the members of their respective departments share the same ideological position.

Threats to Academic Freedom

The pressures on academic freedom originating outside the academy are sometimes exaggerated. Most men of good will are extremely reticent to lend their support to any thoroughgoing censorship over ideas on the campus. The danger to academic freedom is perhaps less likely to result from public concern over what is being taught on campus than from increased control of the purse strings by governmental and quasi-governmental agencies. This very real threat to academic freedom, especially in research, is rooted in the use of tax monies in the manipulation of higher education. This important matter will be further discussed a bit later in the context of public versus private financing of education. Let it suffice here to mention the serious threat of government control in higher education both directly, through subsidy of education with tax money, and indirectly, through agencies holding government contracts.

Though quick to complain of external threats to their academic freedom, professors seldom look to themselves, to the academic community itself, as the source of the trouble. As a case in point, consider the decline in standards which often has accompanied the mass production techniques of modern higher education:

> To want to extend the boundaries of knowledge, or to conserve the wisdom of ancestors, some faith in the importance of learning, and in a Good that is more than private gain, is required. That lacking, the teacher becomes a hired hand, paid to do a chore. . . . The automobile-worker on the assembly line enjoys no special freedom; he has no duties which require a special freedom. And if the teacher willingly assists in the reduction of formal education to a mere degree-mill intended to keep young people very mildly occupied, as if they were in an inordinately expensive kindergarten, then he surely will lose his academic freedom. . . .

Just what sort of academic freedom do these professor-employees expect? And just what sort do they deserve? What sacred trust are they guarding? Just how much do they themselves care about Truth? Some of them have on their shelves no books but a few free copies of textbooks; some of them talk, when they meet together, only of salaries and faculty scandals; some of them say that this state of affairs is a positive good, and look forward with relish to the demise of private foundations which, with intellectual snobbery, still cling to standards.[1]

---

[1] Russell Kirk, *Academic Freedom,* pp. 163, 177.

Academic freedom is further endangered from within by the growing tendency to substitute slogans for thought. Examples of such slogans abound. Appeals for increased emphasis upon proper training of individuals and higher standards within education are often denounced by teacher and administrator alike as "undemocratic." Secure in tenure, many professors seem more irritated than stimulated by a student with an inquiring mind or a colleague who holds differing views. Nicholas Berdyaev might have been addressing himself to the American scene when he remarked: "With sorrow we must recognize the fact that freedom is dear only to those men who think creatively. It is not very necessary to those who do not value thinking."[2]

With due allowance to the many creative thinkers and teachers throughout American education, the truth of Russell Kirk's severe indictment remains:

> Though they may go through the motions of "research," they care precious little about the duty to extend the boundaries of knowledge, and not very much about the duty to conserve the knowledge of our civilization. The humiliating pressure which many administrators endeavor to exert upon teachers to *publish*—to publish just anything, anywhere, for the sake of the record—or to draw up enormous committee-reports about trivialities suggests that both administrators and teachers are ignorant of the true nature of academic freedom and academic dignity. All the administrator wants is some tangible evi-

---

[2] Nicholas Berdyaev, *The Realm of Spirit and The Realm of Caesar*, p. 110.

dence of busy-work to present to his trustees or to the
state legislature; all the teacher wants is some sham-
proof of his liveliness of mind that may bring him a two-
hundred-dollar increase in salary. How much freedom do
such men have? And how much do they deserve?[3]

Political Activism

In addition to those who misinterpret academic freedom
as a "freedom to do nothing," higher education is also faced
with political activists who use their positions as a sanctuary from which politically motivated attacks can be
launched against the rest of society. "Sanctuary" is a well-
advised term. Such political activists never question the
justice of their attacks, yet are the first to raise the cry of
"academic freedom" over the inevitable reaction to their
activity.

Learned Hand once remarked, "You cannot wear a sword
beneath a scholar's gown." He was quite right. No one can
simultaneously be advocate and scholar. Refusal to face this
fact makes the political activist on the campus a primary
offender against the academic freedom he constantly evokes.

Much of the student unrest on campus is directly traceable to faculty agitation, in which a privileged academic
position is used to subvert the entire process. Such professors are often so busy in such causes that they neglect the
very teaching and research which is the reason for the
academic community's existence. Unless the teacher fulfills his duties to the system and convinces society he is dis-

---

[3] Russell Kirk, *Academic Freedom*, p. 162.

charging those duties, he can expect to lose the privileged base he has been granted. Academic freedom is not some irrevocable grant. If it is lost, we all suffer, because the process of creative thinking suffers as does the development of truly free, inner-directed students. But any right is doomed unless its inevitably accompanying responsibilities are discharged.

While the professor has every right to take part in politics on his own, the current tendency to use the academy as an arsenal and staging ground for political combat is both unwarranted and dangerous. Considering the enormous overextension of government in our society, we may expect that when the academy is willing to lend itself to indoctrination and activism rather than education, the end result will be political regulation of that indoctrination. The state will prove to be a poor guardian of academic freedom.

The need is great for the academic community to put its own house in order. The image and the fact of an intellectual community devoted to pursuing the truth must be renewed. Meanwhile, the number of genuine teachers and scholars quietly pursuing their proper function is the cement which still holds the system together, despite all the destructive forces at work upon it.

This community of scholars needs protection on two fronts: from those outside the academy who would destroy freedom through excessive regulation, and from those inside the academy who would destroy the system through license. Unless faculties can regulate themselves from within, they may rest assured they will be regulated from without.

The central question remains then, "Academic Freedom for What?" The answer is two-fold: the pursuit of truth; and the simultaneous responsibility for developing individual students so self-disciplined, so internally free as the result of their knowledge of civilized standards and human responsibilities, that the core of values constituting civilization will be consistently reflected in their behavior. That is the road to salvation not only for the academic community, but for everyone in society. In a word, academic freedom is the freedom to perform the task peculiar to proper education. When the academic community takes other roles unto itself, it does so at the dual risk of failing in its own function while tempting other elements in society to usurp and corrupt the educational function.

10. Revolt on Campus

No OCCURRENCE in contemporary society has attracted more attention than the turmoil in our colleges and universities. The uproar has been accompanied by a rash of hand-wringing and soul-searching; education, the shibboleth of modern America, seems to be disintegrating. When the answer to all problems itself becomes a problem, where does one turn?

For a start, we might examine the psychology of the leadership likely to arise in a revolutionary atmosphere. If we can understand the motivation behind a movement, we should be well on the way to understanding the movement itself. Who is likely to be in the vanguard of an attempt to remake society?

> A man is likely to mind his own business when it is worth minding. When it is not, he takes his mind off his own meaningless affairs by minding other people's business.
>
> This minding of other people's business expresses itself in gossip, snooping and meddling, and also in feverish interest in communal, national and racial affairs. In running away from ourselves we either fall on our neighbor's shoulder or fly at his throat.[1]

---

[1] Eric Hoffer, *The True Believer*, p. 23.

Those who are successful in the affairs of this world tend to be attuned to the reality of *life as it is,* thus disqualifying themselves for visionary leadership. Conversely, in Eric Hoffer's words, "Failure in the management of practical affairs seems to be a qualification for success in the management of public affairs. . . . [Some men] when suffering defeat in the practical world do not feel crushed but are suddenly fired with the apparently absurd conviction that they are eminently competent to direct the fortunes of the community and the nation."[2]

Do the outpourings of a Mario Savio represent the pursuit of power as a means of personal fulfillment? Could the romance of revolution at least partially be explained as an escape from a sense of personal inadequacy? Does the constant escalation of radical student "demands" suggest that men run farthest and fastest when they run from themselves?

When men or nations get tired of dodging fundamental questions in a multitude of distractions, they turn to a search for something else that will, so they suppose, give them the sense of significance which they know they lack. This does not necessarily mean, however, that in sophistication they learn wisdom. If they remain adolescent in their approach to life they are frequently tempted to seek meaning for themselves and for their nation in terms of coercive power. They develop a Messianic complex. They seek to live other people's lives for them, ostensibly for the good of those other people but really in the hope of

---

[2] *Ibid.,* p. 74.

fulfilling themselves. They set out to attain greatness by imposing their supposedly superior understanding upon some man or nation who is less perceptive[3]

Self-Control Abandoned

Irving Babbitt perceived long before most men that modern education was moving down a dangerous path. He noted some 40 years ago that in response to a questionnaire a majority of women's college graduates had rated love of humanity a higher virtue than self-control. Commenting that such a view of human nature might be pardonable in a young woman just out of college, he asked, "What are we to think of our present leaders of public opinion who apparently hold a similar view? Let a man first show that he can act on himself, there will then be time enough for him to act on other men and on the world."[4]

The lapse of self-control in favor of the "humanitarian" view of life partially explains how the dreamer of utopian schemes menaces civilization. While all such revolutionaries share a willingness to destroy the existing order, their ideas of what should be erected in its place tend to vary from vision to vision, reflecting not merely a pipe dream untouched by reality, but a series of pipe dreams as unstable as the personality of the dreamer. Once self-control is abandoned and reality rejected, all that remains are half-formed, bizarre visions of typically unfulfilled revolutionary personalities.

[3] Bernard Iddings Bell, *Crisis in Education,* p. 20.

[4] Irving Babbitt, *Literature and the American College,* p. 47.

Such fuzziness in goals, such lack of personal fulfillment within the existing order, are both evident in the rhetoric of the New Left.

However fuzzy the goals of the New Left may be as to detail, these revolutionaries always envision a future in which the collectivity is endowed with unlimited sovereignty over the individual, all in the name of "social utility." For all the discussion of "freedom," today's campus radicals are quite willing to apply massed force and harassment to intimidate anyone with the temerity to hold opposing views.

> They who clamor loudest for freedom are often the ones least likely to be happy in a free society. The frustrated, oppressed by their shortcomings, blame their future on existing restraints. Actually their innermost desire is for an end to the "free for all." They want to eliminate free competition and the ruthless testing to which the individual is continually subjected in a free society.[5]

This distrust of freedom, this unwillingness to allow others the free expression of their ideas, is woven into the fabric of modern intellectual life. One would be hard put to remember a time in American history when intellectuals were less tolerant than now of one another's ideas. Denunciation, not debate, seems the order of the day. As the Chancellor of the New School, Dr. Harry Gideonse, has remarked, "A few short years ago, anti-intellectualism was an epithet of derogation. Today it is an expression of revolutionary virility." Perhaps part of the reason why so many professors

---

[5] Eric Hoffer, *The True Believer*, p. 37.

have accepted the violent and abusive tactics of the New Left is that such a revolutionary situation offers disgruntled academic oldsters a vicarious opportunity to play the man of action.

The Hard-core Campus Radical

The campus radicals of the New Left pose a mass of contradictions: peace-loving advocates of mob violence; freedom-loving seekers after power; the first to cry "brutality" at any attempted defense against *their* aggressions. The radicals in question are not in university residence to learn—they are there to instruct the university and society. Their qualification? Judging from the public statements of their leadership, to be qualified one must know almost nothing of history, philosophy, economics, or political theory, must have a literary background deeply steeped in James Joyce, Allen Ginsberg, and other purveyors of the four-letter word, and must be constitutionally unable to construct intelligible English prose.

Many observers have remarked upon the strong resemblance between the militant students advocating a new order in Hitler's Germany and the militant students who form the hard core of the New Left. Both have relied upon the demonstration, the use of massed force; both have insisted that "talk" must end, that "action" be the order of the day. In fact, there is much evidence to suggest that the New Left is not really so new. Professor Brzezinski of Columbia University views the current student rebel as essentially counterrevolutionary—i.e., dedicated to the preservation of a dying order. If so, the New Left can be described as the frenzied expression of a "Liberal" intellectual bankruptcy carried to its logical conclusion.

A substantial minority of faculty members lend their support to the New Left disruption of the campus. The professorial pleas for amnesty, the faculty insistence that the rioting students "have a case," is a reflection of the enmity which many academy spokesmen have borne for our essentially free and capitalist-oriented society. Recalling that enmity, that vested interest in the destruction of the old order shared by the Old Left and the New Left, we can discover new meaning in much of the current faculty permissiveness toward the New Left disruptions. We should remember that it was the chairman of the faculty executive committee at Columbia who supported Mark Rudd, among others, with the criticism that the school was run "like a seventeenth or eighteenth century private university." (One wonders exactly what is wrong with *that*. Perhaps the vestiges of academic and disciplinary standards were his grounds for complaint.)

Rejection of the Old Left

However sympathetic the Old Left may be to the antics of the New Left, agreeing in principle and only criticizing the method, it is far from clear that the New Left returns the affection. The ideas of the current campus radicals were formed in the classrooms of Old Left professors, but now it seems that the Old Left itself has been swept over in the rush toward nihilism and destruction.

The Center for the Study of Democratic Institutions recently invited a group of student radicals to Santa Barbara to conduct a "dialogue" on "Students and Society," apparently expecting that an exchange of ideas would reveal grounds for mutual respect and cooperation. However much the Senior Fellows of the Center may have respected their younger partners in the "dialogue," the resultant discussion suggests that the students had something far more radical in mind than did the professors. As one student remarked toward the close of the three-day conference:

> I'm not as angry about what went on as Levine [another student participant] is because when I came here I thought it'd be a lot like going into my grandfather's house. I expected to meet a lot of nice old people who are very interested in what the young are doing and I expected them to tell us that we have a lot of youthful enthusiasm and that that is good, but that there ain't going to be no revolution because when I was 15 years old I said the same thing and there weren't no revolution then and there's going to be no revolution now.
>
> But there is going to be a revolution. I don't know whether you are going to live to see it or not —I hope that you don't, because I don't think you are ready for it. You hope that conscience is built into the existing society, because you can't possibly envision any other kind. I hate to get into this bag of saying that everybody can't understand, but I think it's really true that after the age of 50 you are lost. You people really are far, far out of it—so far that every one of us has had to go on to points in the discussions we had five years ago, just to bring you people

up to where we are today. You've been sitting in this really groovy place called the Center for the Study of Democratic Institutions and you don't know what's going on in the world. I don't think you'll ever understand. I didn't come here to talk to you, though I'm willing to put up with this session. I came here to talk to the other students, because that's where it's at.[6]

The New Left seems to reject dependence upon "dialogue." As one student at the conference urged:

I think we must locate a medium between dialogue and revolution. That medium is disruption. Disruption is the one thing our society can't abide. Our institutions are all interrelated, and if one institution is sabotaged, the society can't function properly as a whole. The institution students are connected with is the university. If I may be permitted a ridiculous metaphor, the university is a kind of distributor cap that students can remove from the engine of our society.[7]

Disrupt and Destroy

Disruption and destruction of the existing system seem the new order of the day. The *Berkeley Barb,* a New Left organ in California, typifies such sentiment:

The universities cannot be reformed. They must be abandoned or closed down. They should be used as bases for actions against society, but never taken seriously. The

---

[6] *Students and Society,* Center for the Study of Democratic Institutions, pp. 61-62.

[7] *Ibid.,* p. 43.

professors have nothing to teach. . . . We can learn more
from any jail than we can from any university.

Like most revolutionary appeals, the New Left stresses its
interest in the common needs of all students, urging student unity; but in practice that appeal quickly degenerates
into "Be my brother or I'll kill you," providing us with a
more accurate measure of New Left values. Meanwhile, the
provocations and the "kicks" go on. The attempt to provoke
society becomes not merely the means, but the end as well.
So long as these *provocateurs* remain a comparatively small
minority on campus, a deliberately disruptive group totally
disinterested in education and determined to deny that education to the majority, there is a means of solving that problem. The solution was provided long ago in a letter written
by St. Benedict[8] to instruct his monks in the proper operation of a monastery:

> If any pilgrim monk come from distant parts, if with
> wish as a guest to dwell in the monastery, and will be
> content with the customs which he finds in the place, and
> do not by his lavishness disturb the monastery, but is
> simply content with what he finds, he shall be received,
> for as long a time as he desires. If, indeed he find fault
> with anything, or expose it, reasonably, and with the
> humility of charity, the Abbot shall discuss it prudently,
> lest perchance God had sent him for this very thing. . . .
> But, if he have been found gossipy and contumacious in
> the time of his sojourn as guest, not only ought he not to

---

[8] Much of the same advice is also given by St. Benedict in Chapter
61 of his *Rule for Monasteries*.

be joined to the body of the monastery, but also it shall be said to him, honestly, that he must depart. If he does not go, let two stout monks, in the name of God, explain the matter to him.

Rights of the Majority?

A troublesome point remains. Isn't it true that far more students seem disaffected with higher education than the small group of admittedly New Left radicals? Are all these masses of students actual or potential members of a student revolt dedicated to the disruption of our colleges and universities? The answer to both questions is "yes." Unless we are willing to take a long, hard look at American higher education, we may expect the numbers of disaffected students to continue their growth.

While most American college youths are far more interested in education than in destruction, they do feel betrayed by an educational structure which has become increasingly unresponsive to their academic needs and oppressive to their development as responsible adult individuals. It is this large group of disaffected students that forms the reservoir of discontent exploited by the New Left.

The student attending college for the first time has (or should have) some idea of what a college education is supposed to provide. Most serious students are likely to expect intellectual discipline and high standards, not to mention a close working relationship between teacher and pupil. For the student, these disciplines, standards, and relationships presumably will provide the development of individual capacity and judgment, making for a well-formed and uniquely individual personality. So much for the expectations of the serious student; the realities are often painfully different.

A Bureaucratic Merry-Go-Round

The uses of the multiversity for fund-raising, for the aggrandizement of administration and faculty, and for mass student indoctrination, all militate against proper education for the individual. Today a college education is automatic (and often meaningless). Insert a six-year-old in the educational mill and sixteen years later he is a college graduate, whether or not he has learned anything of lasting value or has matured into a unique and self-reliant personality. Such an overinstitutionalized and de-individualized system becomes primarily custodial in nature. Often this custodial function is highly paternal, but that very paternalism becomes the greatest despotism of all. The bureaucracy necessitated by such overinstitutionalized education becomes self-perpetuating, and steadily less devoted to the functions of genuine education.

While such a bureaucracy can no longer educate, it lends itself admirably well to social engineering, to turning out technically proficient automatons ideally suited to running "the system" without questioning its values. This is one of the valid complaints our students have. One of the bits of doggerel of the Berkeley uprising, to be sung to Beethoven's Ninth Symphony, went as follows:

> From the tip of San Diego,
>   to the top of Berkeley's hills
> We have built a mighty factory,
>   to impart our social skills.
> Social engineering triumph,
>   managers of every kind
> Let us all with drills and homework
>   manufacture human minds!

Thus, a moulding process is often substituted for an educational process. The students who are caught in the gears
of the multiversity are to be excused for the feeling that the
individual is powerless to change his environment. And, if
the individual no longer matters, perhaps massive action,
action designed to disrupt the workings of the existing system, is the only answer.

A related problem centers on the fact that many of our
young people are more concerned than previous generations to know the "reason why," to examine the moral
premises of our society. Perhaps they hunger for this because our present educational structure offers them so few
values and principles on which to build their lives. Whatever the reason, the student with this concern for moral
issues often finds himself in the company of professors for
whom the morality of the existing power structure is a
matter of little or no interest.

When the student does find a professor who is at least
willing to discuss ultimate moral questions, such a professor
all too often proves to be an activist who foments just the
sort of campus revolt advocated by the New Left. A pro-

fessor at Berkeley described the faculty-student relationship at the time of the 1964 Free Speech Movement:

> ... So far as I was able to judge, the vast majority of the undergraduates did their best to follow the confused and changing lead of their professors.[9]

Thus, the riots have often epitomized the breakdown in traditional values, a breakdown deliberately induced by some faculty members. Could it be that our society's unwillingness to honor our own traditions is undercutting our young people's capacity to honor anything? If so, we should not be surprised when more and more of our youth no longer wish to play the game.

Much of our present structure of higher education offers the spectacle of teachers unwilling to teach, operating within an overinstitutionalized educational structure which smothers the individual student. The system, for all its size and power, so lacks inner values that it is often unable to act even in self-defense when assaulted by New Left revolutionaries from within. Surely such a system has little claim to the loyalties of the majority of sincere students who come to college to get an education!

Perhaps the New Left minority and the disaffected student majority are but different symptoms of the same disease. Perhaps they are all young people who in varying degrees are being robbed of their personalities and their core of civilizing values by a morally bankrupt educational structure badly in need of revision.

---

[9] William Peterson, "What's Lost at Berkeley," *Columbia University Forum* (Spring, 1965), p. 39.

11. Creativity

"THE CHIEF WONDER OF EDUCATION is that it does not ruin everybody connected with it, teachers and taught," Henry Adams once remarked. Such may indeed be the sad consequence of an education that fails to teach people to think, to participate in some small way in the creative process which distinguishes man from animal.

If we would better understand the creative process, we might begin with the recognition that creativity does not originate in and cannot be measured by standardized controls. The concepts of standardization and creativity are mutually exclusive. Our society's continuing attempt to judge its success by the degree of "consensus" it achieves, by the extent to which it imposes "adjustment" on the individuals who are its members, is a demonstration of our failure to realize the mutually exclusive nature of that relationship. We seem to insist that the individual will find fulfillment to the extent that he makes his peace with the system.

It is true enough that we must be able to live and work with our fellows. But, is mere "adjustment" enough? A *Fortune* study undertaken a few years ago asked 150 corporation presidents and 150 personnel directors whether, if they *had* to choose, they would prefer: (1) the adaptable administrator, skilled in managerial techniques and concerned primarily with human relations and with making the corporation a smooth-working team; or (2) a man with strong personal convictions who is not shy about making decisions likely to upset tested procedures. The vote: the presidents divided half-and-half; the personnel men, 3-to-1 in favor of the administrator.[1] This preference for "adjustment" over creative leadership is widespread in our society.

When creative capacity is sacrificed to adjustment, the results are likely to be futile and uninspiring. In fact, human beings owe most of their conspicuous historical advances to periods when "adjustment" and control could not be forced upon social life. The dead hand of conformity and spontaneous forces of creativity simply do not act in concert. The periods historians usually describe as "civilized" were invariably triggered by lapses of enforced conformity, thus making possible a creative flowering.

There can be no such thing as "creativity on command," because genuine originality arises within the individual, not the collectivity. That aristocratic element in creativity implies a reliance upon higher standards than can be expected of society as a whole. The personal aspect of creativity cannot be mass-produced. Indeed, the process works in reverse. Confucius had the idea that if an individual

---

[1] William H. Whyte, Jr., "The New Illiteracy," *The Public Schools in Crisis,* ed. by Mortimer Smith, p. 108.

could only come to terms with his own personality and develop his own potential, that development would extend, in ever-widening circles, throughout a larger and larger area of influence, first touching those nearest the individual, finally spreading to the community at large. Since societies on the whole have proven notoriously unwilling to accept high standards and truly advanced ideas, the result of such individual creative development, when it has occurred, has been the apparent "social maladjustment" of the unique and creative personality, whose only guilt consists in his possessing more wisdom than society can accept. When societies have chosen to penalize such "maladjustment" and have demanded conformity, they often have destroyed the creative impulses which gave them viability.

Creation in the Service of Truth

Thus, society is obligated to allow freedom to the creative individual or risk its own destruction. A form of that same obligation applies to the creative individual. Unless his capacities are used to serve truth, the creative individual is also finally destroyed. Those who live immediately *after* a period of free creativity are especially vulnerable in this regard. Because previous creative genius has already "thought through" a problem, subsequent generations often feel it unnecessary to rethink it, thus failing to recreate the solution within themselves. Few men have realized that the true must be not only discovered, but perennially *rediscovered* and *redefined*. Any moral code which does not allow for individual, internal *expansion* of an ethical ideal is doomed to extinction. In Ortega's words, "the good is, like nature, an immense landscape in which man advances through centuries of exploration."[2]

There are signs that the modern world displays little enthusiasm for advance along such lines. We seem to feel that we can free the whole world from material concerns, but one need ask, "What does it profit a man to free the whole world if his soul is not free?"[3]

And how free are our souls if we are valued by the world around us only for our ability to shed our personalities, to "adapt" to the values and standards of our society, to suffer the death and burial of the originality and creative capacity which should give us our identities?

In this world of utilitarian and materialist values, we seem to have forgotten that truth is not the servant of man. Unless the individual is the servant of truth, both he and his society are doomed. Society cannot do without the services of the creative individual; the creative individual is likewise doomed unless his capacities serve a higher morality than his own devising. The individual achieves his fulfillment only as he overcomes his own limitations and transcends himself in service of a higher ideal.

> . . . If there is no God, as Truth and Meaning, if there is no higher Justice, then everything flattens out, and there is neither any one nor any thing to which man can rise. If on the other hand, man is God, the situation is flatter

---

[2] José Ortega y Gasset, *Meditations*, p. 37.

[3] George Santayana, *Character and Opinion in the United States,* p. 118.

still, hopeless and worthless. Every qualitative value is an indication that in the path of man's life there lies something higher than man. And that which is higher than man, i.e., the divine, is not an exterior force standing above and ruling him, but that which, in him, makes him truly man—his higher freedom.[4]

The Key to Creation

True education must recognize the individual nature of originality and creativity. No matter how dynamic the teacher, the effective force in genuine education is the student's will to learn and to grow. All learning and discovery, with or without a teacher, takes place deep in the individual's personality. Sir Isaac Newton, when asked how he had reduced the vast quantity of physical phenomena to apparent simplicity, replied, *Nocte dieque incubando* (turning them over day and night). The one fact which we know about that "turning" process is that it demanded a tremendous withdrawal into self, tremendous thought and introspection.

To compare Newton's answer with the methods all too common in modern academic research provides a revealing insight. First the researcher "structures" a research project, gathers a team of co-workers, and requests foundation grants in support of his work—then, if the corporate judgment so wills it, the "team project" begins. That such research provides "facts," one cannot deny. It is less clear

---

[4] Nicholas Berdyaev, *The Realm of Spirit and the Realm of Caesar,* p. 40.

that it yields the intuitive perceptions which can be
achieved when a gifted individual takes those facts and
"turns them over day and night."

The collective approach to wisdom is forever suspect.
Emerson once insisted:

> Ours is the age of the omnibus, of the third person
> plural, of Tammany Hall. Is it that Nature has only so
> much vital force, and must dilute it if it is to be multi-
> plied into millions? The beautiful is never plentiful.[5]

"The beautiful is never plentiful." How true. When we
complain of the "failures of our age," do we not label ourselves unrealistic? Haven't all ages and all societies been
filled with shortcomings? The great achievements have always been individualistic. Indeed, any original achievement
implies separation from the majority. Though society may
honor achievement, it can never produce it.

The morning after Charles Lindbergh flew the Atlantic
nonstop from New York to Paris, an associate of Charles
Kettering rushed into the research expert's laboratory in
Dayton, Ohio, shouting: "He made it! Lindbergh landed
safely in Paris!" Kettering went on working. The associate
spoke again: "Think of it—Lindbergh flew the Atlantic
alone! He did it all by himself!" Kettering looked up from
his work momentarily and remarked quietly: "When he
flies it with a committee, let me know."

It seems as if the Deity dressed each soul which he

---

[5] *Emerson: A Modern Anthology,* ed. by Alfred Kazin and Daniel
Aaron, p. 182.

sends into nature in certain virtues and powers not communicable to other men, and sending it to perform one
more turn through the circle of beings, wrote, *"Not trans-
ferable"* and *"Good for this trip only,"* on these garments
of the soul. There is something deceptive about the intercourse of minds. The boundaries are invisible, but they
are never crossed.[6]

If each of us is to perform his unique function, each must
be free to do so. The word "freedom" means nothing unless
it consists first of all in freedom of personality, the individuality possible only if a person is a free creative spirit
over whom neither state nor society is omnipotent. The
individual must be free to listen to that still small voice
within:

> There is a time in every man's education when he ar-
> rives at the conviction that envy is ignorance; that imi-
> tation is suicide; that he must take himself for better or
> worse as his portion; that though the wide universe is
> full of good, no kernel of nourishing corn can come to
> him but through his toil bestowed on that plot of ground
> which is given to him to till. The power which resides
> in him is new in nature, and none but he knows what
> that is which he can do, nor does he know until he has
> tried.[7]

The individual who is thus cultivating his own little piece
of the universe may well be engaged in the production of a

---

6 *Ibid.,* p. 215.

7 *Ibid.,* p. 99.

unique and valuable vision, a vision which no collection of men, no "consensus" can possibly evaluate:

> . . . the only difference is that what many see we call a real thing, and what only one sees we call a dream. But things that many see may have no taste or moment in them at all, and things that are shown only to one may be spears and water-spouts of truth from the very depth of truth.[8]

These "water-spouts of truth from the very depth of truth" are the product of individual intuition. Such intuition operates largely outside the conscious mind. It goes under many names and is subject to many interpretations, ranging from "a flash of insight into Absolute Truth" to "promptings from a guardian angel." Those who are responsive to such promptings are the creative among us. Probably many more of us might participate in Creation if we would only respond to our intuitions, if we would fan the tiny spark into a flame. Unless we leave the individual free to do that job for himself, unless we prepare him for such an expectation, we do not have an educational system worth its name.

The Role of a Demanding Environment

Granted the necessity for intuition, how does a man learn to discipline himself and respond to the call when it comes? Imagination there must be, but imagination disciplined by intellect. The development of intellect demands work and academic standards. Only an education with a well-de-

---

[8] C. S. Lewis, *Till We Have Faces*, p. 277.

veloped hierarchy of values, demanding much from the individual, can lay the groundwork for the union of imagination and intellect which allows creative thinking.

What are some of the elements in such a hierarchy of values? One necessary element would be a well-developed memory—reminding the world that lasting accomplishment is produced not by the easily-pleased forgetter of hard truths, but by the man who remembers and understands reality, even when it is most painful. Another element would be a well-established set of values which the individual has accepted as his own. A distinguished psychiatrist has recently made it clear that sound character formation is not possible unless the individual clearly knows who he is and what he believes.[9] Here again, lasting accomplishment has never come from those willing to shift their personality or their principles for a more comfortable "adjustment" with the world. Accomplishment, intuition, and creativity have always come from those who knew who they were and what they believed, even when they suffered at the hands of the world for their firm grasp of reality and personal identity.

Self-Esteem

Such creative people, knowing who they are and what they value, tend to reflect self-esteem. A recent study of self-esteem among young boys reflected a high correlation between what the boys did and what they *thought* they

9 William Glasser, *Mental Health or Mental Illness?*, p. 15.

142

EDUCATION IN AMERICA

could do. Those boys coming from homes where parents maintained a close interest in them, where parents demanded high standards of behavior and performance, where firm discipline was a fact, not a debating point, proved to be boys of strength and achievement, capable of creative application of intellect, personality, and imagination.

The findings from these studies concerning the factors that contribute to the formation of high self-esteem suggest important implications for parents, educators, and therapists. They indicate that children develop self-trust, venturesomeness, and the ability to deal with adversity if they are treated with respect and are provided with well-defined standards of value, demands for competence, and guidance toward solutions of problems. It appears that the development of independence and self-reliance is fostered by a well-structured, demanding environment rather than by largely unlimited permissiveness and freedom to explore in an unfocused way.[10]

Just as the individual must be free to pursue his intuition, so he must be the product of a disciplined environment to develop properly his capacities of intellect and imagination. Once again, those interested in education are faced with the necessity of providing freedom for the individual to choose, but defining it as freedom to choose within an already established framework of values. It appears to be true that

---

[10] Stanley Coopersmith, "Studies in Self-Esteem," *Scientific American,* Feb. 1968, p. 106.

man can only be genuinely free when he accepts the discipline of a higher standard. Perhaps each of us can only be a creator to the extent that we are in harmony with The Creator.

The man who lives his own vocation and follows his own destiny is the creative man, since his life is in full agreement with his true self. It is the business of education to allow the individual to develop that harmony of capacity and opportunity, of intent and fulfillment, of creativity and creation, which provides the chance for the individual to use his life in pursuit of everlasting goals and achievements.

12. A Philosophy of Growth

IN THIS EXAMINATION of education in America, we find substantial gaps between the ideal we envision and the reality we face. Closing those gaps by constructing a comprehensive educational "system" seems unrealistic, not only because it is difficult to focus any system upon the individual, but also because society rejects any such attempt. We must remember, however, that the process of education is epitomized by ceaseless questioning, even when the answers seem difficult or distant. In the best sense of education, each of us must ask, and finally answer, his own questions. Ethical considerations, in the final analysis, are matters of individual conscience. Unless each of us is free to ask and answer the proper questions, matters of ethical import can hardly be considered, much less decided.

Furthermore, none of us can accurately gauge the mind of another. Those with least apparent promise often come forth with astounding creativity. Education must offer challenge and variety to awaken the individual conscience and draw forth unique qualities and capacities. Looking for the best in others and allowing their free development, *letting people be themselves,* affords each the opportunity

144

to achieve his own potential. Such a view of education implies no "system," no "establishment," in the usual sense.

The central fact of our present educational structure is its failure to allow for individuality. Increasingly institutionalized education emphasizes the collectivity over the individual, denies the significance of religious sanction in the lives of men, insists upon relativity as the highest standard of morality. The result has been a lowering of standards and an erosion of the dignity and worth of the individual—the very antithesis of genuine education.

The Aim of Education

The task of the educator is primarily that of *liberation*. The individual needs to be freed from his limitations in order to develop his potentialities and become a better man than he would otherwise have been. This is the most radical presumption of all. If we assume that the individual can develop his unique potentialities only in freedom, implicit in that assumption is that different people have different capacities and varying rates of progress. Thus, genuine education implies discrimination and difference as distinguished from the dead level of equality.

Once this individual quality of education is understood, it becomes apparent that "social utility" is not an appropriate measure of the student's achievement. Respect for the individual requires that his education be measured in terms of his growth, his *becoming*. The object and the measure of genuine education remains the individual. Development of individual personality, not social conformity, should be education's concern. Education is the process by which the individual gains possession of his soul and becomes a human being fully responsive to his capacities.

In a practical sense, genuine education trains students to *think for themselves*. Mere indoctrination will not suffice:

> Cannot we let people be themselves, and enjoy life in their own way? You are trying to make that man another *you*. One's enough.[1]

If education is to provide the opportunity for the full development of personality and independent thought, it must also provide a frame of reference giving meaning to that independence. Reverence for truth is quite as important as development of personal uniqueness. Thoreau's remark that "in the long run men hit only what they aim at," should serve to remind us that education must also give status and direction to man's moral existence, convincing the individual that man *is* more than merely animal and therefore possesses correspondingly higher obligations and aspirations.

We may now define in a more precise manner the aim of education. It is to guide man in the evolving dynamism through which he shapes himself as a human person—armed with knowledge, strength of judgment, and moral virtues—while at the same time conveying to him the spiritual heritage of the nation and the civilization in

---

[1] *Emerson: A Modern Anthology,* ed. by Alfred Kazin and Daniel Aaron, p. 363.

which he is involved, and preserving in this way the century-old achievements of generations.[2]

Emerson once criticized the utopian quality of his own work, saying, "I found when I had finished my new lecture that it was a very good house, only the architect had unfortunately omitted the stairs." Such a demanding view of education as outlined in these pages runs the risk of being a "house without stairs." Especially in view of the present institutional structure, what educator can perform such a demanding task?

Fortunately, we need not wait for institutional reform if we wish substantially to improve the education of our young. Not all education occurs in the school. Education, like charity, begins at home. If the task of reforming a giant educational structure serving millions of children seems too large, could each of us at least assume responsibility for the proper mental and moral development of a single child? The individual need not feel impotent when he has before him a task on a scale which he *can* comprehend as an individual, especially when that task is the development of human personality, surely the single most important undertaking in the world. There is one catch: If the effort is to have the chance to succeed, the individual educator of the individual child must want to meet the challenge.

. . . people, I am certain, greatly underestimate the power of men to achieve their real choices. But the choices must be real and primary, not secondary, ones.

---

[2] Jacques Maritain, *Education at the Crossroads,* p. 10.

Men will often say that they want such and such a thing, and true, they do want such and such a thing, but it turns out that they want something else more. It is what they want most that they will be most active, ingenious, imaginative, and tireless in seeking. When a person decides that he really wants something, he finds he can surpass himself; he can change circumstances and attain to a goal that in his duller hours seemed unattainable. As an old teacher of mine used to say, "When you have done your utmost, something will be given to you." But first must come the honest desire.[3]

Parental Responsibility

Unfortunately, many parents have been unwilling to assume primary responsibility for their offspring. It is true that the modern school has tended to assume functions for which it was ill-suited, thus becoming a poor substitute for the parent, but the primary blame must rest with the negligence of many parents.

The selfishness of more and more of our contemporary parents also manifests itself in neglect of children. Parents all too often pity themselves, run away from their plain duty, their chief job, their greatest avenue to the respect of God and of honest men. They place their own welfare, even their amusements ahead of the well-being of their sons and daughters. They may, and usually do, see that the boys and girls are clothed, fed, washed, have their teeth attended to; but to make pals of them, to live with

---

[3] Richard Weaver, *Life Without Prejudice,* p. 119.

them, to laugh and cry and work and play with them, lovingly but firmly to discipline them, this takes too much time and effort altogether. The American parent tends increasingly to pamper himself or herself. In consequence little is taught to the children by precept and less by example. Then the parents dump their progeny at the feet of the schoolmaster and schoolmistress and say, "Here, we have no time to bring these youngsters up, nor have we any stomach for the job. You take them over, as totally as possible, and do what we will not do for our own. Train them in character; that is what you get paid for."[4]

Before we can impart self-discipline to our children, we must first possess that quality ourselves. We cannot solve the problem of raising children by pretending to make the schools responsible; nor can we solve the problem of exercising authority by transferring that authority to the children themselves.

Let us have a little severe hard work, good, clean, well-written exercises, well-pronounced words, well-set-down sums: and as far as head-work goes, no more. . . . Let us have a bit of solid, hard, tidy work. . . .

And one must do this to children, not only to love them, but to make them free and proud: If a boy slouches out of a door, throw a book at him, like lightning; don't stand for the degenerate, nervous, twisting, wistful, pathetic centreless children we are cursed with: or the fat and self-satisfied, sheep-in-the-pasture children who are be-

---

[4] Bernard Iddings Bell, *Crisis in Education,* pp. 98-99.

coming more common: or the impudent, I'm-as-good-as-anybody smirking children who are far too numerous.[5]

How many parents would face up to such a responsibility in their own home? How many would tolerate, much less encourage, a school operated on such "old-fashioned" principles? The process of character building is a demanding, day-by-day job. The job implies great expectations in the child, plus the parent's willingness to give the sustained time and effort to insist that the expectation is fulfilled.

Not only must the parent be prepared to give of himself to accomplish the task, but he must be prepared to set the proper example. Does this demand a great deal of each of us? Yes, indeed! And no amount of tax collection and PTA activity can serve as a substitute. Any area of life where we achieve success demands time, energy, patience—expenditure of *self*. Surely the building of a family and the raising of children can be no exception. It is not enough to know what is right; we must also live that knowledge. "If one's wisdom exceeds one's deeds, the wisdom will not endure." This is a highly individual task, one which cannot be successfully collectivized.

Does such parental responsibility rule out the importance of the teacher? Indeed not. The dedicated teacher, who has mastered himself and who would spend his life in helping the young to master their lives, is engaged in one of the highest callings. Without such men and women, the school as an extension of parental responsibility would be impos-

---

[5] G. H. Bantock, *Freedom and Authority in Education*, pp. 175, 177.

sible. In fact, it has been the devotion to duty of many teachers and administrators which has enabled our educational system to keep operating successfully, despite bureaucratic rigidity and parental flight from responsibility. Still, the good teacher is fighting a losing fight unless the home enforces the discipline and standards necessary to support the learning experience of the classroom. Ultimately, failures in education rest with the individual parents who are willing to accept less than the best, and unwilling to fulfill their own responsibilities. Our children finally receive an education which is an accurate reflection of the principles accepted by adult society.

Public Funding of Education

The Bundy Report on urban education, financed by the Ford Foundation, has described the current educational bureaucracy as "a system already grown rigid in its negative powers," and has warned that power and responsibility must go hand in hand. This was to have been achieved by the now famous "decentralization." In practical terms, the results of decentralization in New York City Public Schools have been a resounding failure. The entire nation has watched public education in Ocean Hill-Brownsville literally come to a halt. But this is not the failure of a genuine attempt at decentralization. The people have insisted that schools be publicly funded, and yet pretended that somehow this would not affect the decision-making process in neighborhood schools. Power and responsibility have not been allowed to flow together. The individual parents in

Ocean Hill-Brownsville should have a say in the education
of their children; they also should pay for that education.
So long as they lack that responsibility, it is not surprising
that they act irresponsibly.

Across this nation, those parents who would exercise responsible choice in the education of their children are pe-
nalized for their responsible behavior. Parents who would
place their children in a private school more responsive to
their values and attitudes are advised by the tax collector,
"First support the State's educational philosophy; then, if
you have any surplus resources, you may pursue *your* educational philosophy."

Education in America has become a reflection of the insistence that education be a function of government, cost
free to participating students, fully financed at taxpayer expense. What originated as *local* schooling, supported by tax-
ation in the immediate community (and therefore somewhat
responsive to local and parental wishes) has inexorably
moved toward bureaucratic bigness—the fate of all publicly
funded projects. On the local level, the parent finds the
system less and less responsive to his concerns. Meanwhile,
power has tended to gravitate from the little red school-
house to the State House and from the State House to Wash-
ington. Control of the purse strings has brought control of
education.

The remaining private educational institutions on all levels face exorbitant costs as they try to compete for scarce
educational resources. How are they to attract students and
faculty in view of the expensive plants, research facilities,

salary scales, and subsidized tuition offered by "public" institutions? Many have succumbed to the lure of state and Federal aid, losing self-control in the process.

There have been various proposals for relief of this bureaucratic congestion, among them the idea of "decentralization." But recent events should make it clear that no genuine decentralization can occur under public funding. The effect of socialized finance in any project, education included, is toward more centralized control, not less.

Another proposal is to allow the individual tax credit for income spent or given for educational purposes. This, too, might serve as a holding action, though it still fails to deal with the underlying moral issue. Why should the money of one citizen be taken by force to finance the education of other peoples' children, any more than to finance the building of other peoples' homes, the gasoline for other peoples' cars, the payment of other peoples' medical expenses? I have yet to hear a compelling *moral* argument justifying coercion for such a purpose.

So long as we are willing to allow an immoral premise to dominate our educational endeavors, we must be willing to live with ugly results. The only lasting solution is to remove education from the hands of government, restoring responsibility to the student and the parent.

The response at that point tends to be, "Why, if there were no public education, parents wouldn't send their children to school!" I have yet to meet the person who will not send *his* children to school. It is always those *other people* who would supposedly be remiss in their duty. A parallel case may be discovered in the arguments of the last century concerning organized religion. The original argument for a state-supported church was that religion would fail if people were given their choice whether or not to support organized religion. The identical argument is advanced today in regard to education, despite the fact that religion thrives after more than a century of separation of church from state. Is there any compelling reason why voluntary support of education should not be given a similar opportunity?

Ultimate Solutions

Educational reform must begin with parents as individuals, with the recognition that better upbringing for their children lies in their hands, not in the hands of the state. If and when enough parents begin living their lives self-responsibly and apply such principles to their children who are an extension of self, a new educational day will have dawned. The answer, then, is not to "throw the rascals out," substituting good men for bad in the political control of collectivized education. Instead, let each act in his own small orbit, with his own children, with those whom he influences directly. If one's example and understanding are of high enough quality, the educational picture will begin to change *no matter what course politicalized education might take*.

Those who effect great revolutions are always small in number. Such people need not wait to become a majority. No one else *can* do the job except those who understand what needs to be done. The disruptive influence of political centralization in education will continue until it has been overshadowed and rendered meaningless by a moral force of sufficient intensity, a force generated by individuals who understand what is at stake and who serve notice by their own example that a better way exists to educate our young.

Index of Authors

Prepared by Vernelia A. Crawford

This index includes the titles of chapters listed under the appropriate subject classification. With the exception of these specific pages, which are hyphenated, the numbers in each instance refer to the *first* page of a discussion. A page number followed by the letter "n" indicates the number of a footnote reference. An Index of Subjects follows this Index of Authors.

158

Hook, Sidney, 109, 114
Hutchins, Robert, 9, 42n, 68n, 99, 101n
Huxley, Julian, 48

James, Henry, 41
Joad, C. E. M., 40

Kazin, Alfred, ed., 138n, 146n
Kerr, Clark, 96, 97
Kettering, Charles, 138
Kirk, Russell, 115n, 116, 117n
Krech, David, 31n
Krutch, Joseph Wood, 31, 41

Lewis, C. S., 15, 19n, 26, 33, 36, 45, 46n, 49n, 140n
Lindbergh, Charles, 138
Linton, Calvin D., 63n, 77n

Mann, Thomas, 41
Maritain, Jacques, 21n, 51n, 52n, 147n
Molnar, Thomas, 15n, 49n, 55n, 102n, 107n
More, Paul Elmer, 26

Newman, John Henry, 30
Newton, Isaac, 137
Nietzsche, Friedrich, 79
Nock, Albert Jay, 25, 58

O'Neill, Eugene, 34

Ortega y Gasset, José, 22n, 35, 38, 39n, 51n, 55, 103n, 136

Peacock, Thomas, 1
Peterson, William, 132n
Pieper, Josef, 37, 38n, 102
Plato, 16, 17, 20, 37
Pound, Ezra, 41
Proust, Marcel, 41

Rousseau, Jean Jacques, 60
Rudd, Mark, 23, 125

St. Benedict, 128
St. Paul, 17
St. Thomas, 37, 51
Santayana, George, 136n
Savio, Mario, 23, 121
Schaar, John H., 98n
Schrag, Peter, 31n
Schuyler, George, 34
Schweitzer, Albert, 7
Sinsheiner, Robert, 32
Smith, J. Allen, 36
Smith, Mortimer, 76, 134n

Thoreau, Henry David, 146
Tocqueville, Alexis de, 57

Weaver, Richard, 3n, 15, 53, 57n, 90, 148n
Weir, John, 48
Whyte, William H., 134n
Wolin, Sheldon S., 98n
Wordsworth, Henry, 18

Index of Subjects

159

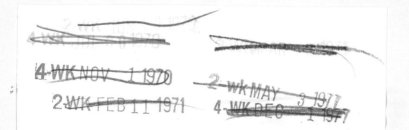

2 WK NOV 1 1970

4 WK NOV 1 1970

2 WK FEB 11 1971

2 wk MAY 3 1977

4 WK DEC 1 1977

2 wk JAN 3 1978

2 WK FEB 26 1975

4 WK SEP 4 1975

2 wk FEB 1 6 1976

2 wk OCT 29 1976

4 WK NOV 2 1977

2 wk AUG 1 6 1978